Cambridge Elements

Elements in Gender and Politics
edited by
Tiffany D. Barnes
University of Texas at Austin
Diana Z. O'Brien
Washington University in St. Louis

ATTITUDES TOWARD POLITICAL AUTHORITARIANISM IN ECONOMICALLY ADVANCED DEMOCRACIES

The Role of Gender Values and Norms

Amy C. Alexander
University of Gothenburg

Gefjon Off
Leuphana University of Lüneburg and University of Hamburg

Shaftesbury Road, Cambridge CB2 8EA, United Kingdom

One Liberty Plaza, 20th Floor, New York, NY 10006, USA

477 Williamstown Road, Port Melbourne, VIC 3207, Australia

314–321, 3rd Floor, Plot 3, Splendor Forum, Jasola District Centre, New Delhi – 110025, India

103 Penang Road, #05–06/07, Visioncrest Commercial, Singapore 238467

Cambridge University Press is part of Cambridge University Press & Assessment, a department of the University of Cambridge.

We share the University's mission to contribute to society through the pursuit of education, learning and research at the highest international levels of excellence.

www.cambridge.org
Information on this title: www.cambridge.org/9781009539371

DOI: 10.1017/9781009374309

© Amy C. Alexander and Gefjon Off 2025

This publication is in copyright. Subject to statutory exception and to the provisions of relevant collective licensing agreements,no reproduction of any part may take place without the written permission of Cambridge University Press & Assessment.

When citing this work, please include a reference to the DOI 10.1017/9781009374309

First published 2025

A catalogue record for this publication is available from the British Library

ISBN 978-1-009-53937-1 Hardback
ISBN 978-1-009-37432-3 Paperback
ISSN 2753-8117 (online)
ISSN 2753-8109 (print)

Additional resources for this publication at www.cambridge.org/EGAP_Alexander

Cambridge University Press & Assessment has no responsibility for the persistence or accuracy of URLs for external or third-party internet websites referred to in this publication and does not guarantee that any content on such websites is, or will remain, accurate or appropriate.

For EU product safety concerns, contact us at Calle de José Abascal, 56, 1°, 28003 Madrid, Spain, or email eugpsr@cambridge.org

Attitudes toward Political Authoritarianism in Economically Advanced Democracies

The Role of Gender Values and Norms

Elements in Gender and Politics

DOI: 10.1017/9781009374309
First published online: June 2025

Amy C. Alexander
University of Gothenburg

Gefjon Off
Leuphana University of Lüneburg and University of Hamburg

Author for correspondence: Amy C. Alexander, amy.alexander@gu.se

Abstract: This Element focuses on how individuals' gender values and populations' gender norms influence their attitudes toward political authoritarianism in economically advanced democracies. First, it theorizes that individuals' higher support for gender equality and freedom of sexuality (GEFS) decreases their support of political authoritarianism. This operates directly through the development of a belief system that is incompatible with political authoritarianism as a system rooted in and sustained through conformity to hegemonic masculine dominance. Additionally, this operates indirectly by strengthening support for pluralism, strengthening support for democratic socialization in households, and increasing rejection of the use of violence to control household social relations. Second, it theorizes how GEFS norms and political authoritarian norms are mutually reinforcing in shaping political culture at the country level. The Element shows evidence consistent with these theories through analysis of data on OECD countries from 1995 to 2022 based on waves 3–7 of the World Values Surveys.

Keywords: political authoritarianism, gender equality, freedom of sexuality, socialization, hegemonic masculinity

© Amy C. Alexander and Gefjon Off 2025

ISBNs: 9781009539371 (HB), 9781009374323 (PB), 9781009374309 (OC)
ISSNs: 2753-8117 (online), 2753-8109 (print)

Contents

Introduction   1

1 A Theory of Individuals' GEFS Values and Their Attitudes toward Political Authoritarianism   5

2 An Analysis of How Individuals' Support of GE and FS Decreases Their Support of Political Authoritarianism   15

3 A Theory of How Countries Develop a Culture of GEFS and Political (Anti-)Authoritarianism as Mutually Reinforcing Cultural Processes   40

4 An Analysis of GEFS Norms and Political (Anti-)Authoritarian Norms as Mutually Reinforcing   54

5 Conclusion   69

References   74

Introduction

More recently, developed, economically advanced democracies such as the United States, Hungary and Poland have observed the rise of political leaders with alarming authoritarian inclinations, followed by the passing of increasingly restrictive women's and LGBTQI+ rights laws. In the United States, examples include overturning the right to abortion, the rise of gender affirming care bans, and bills attempting to censor discussion of gender identities in schools. In Poland, this includes the rise of "LGBT-free zones" and restrictions to the right to abortion. And, in Hungary, this includes changes in the constitution to exclude LGBTQI+ people from the definition of the family and prohibit showing content on LGBTQI+ realities to minors. In addition to these examples, parties that tend to attract and recruit authoritarian-leaning leaders, radical right parties, are ushering in similar proposals as they gain support across various European democracies. To name a few examples, the radical right Freedom Party of Austria (FPÖ) advocates for a "family policy centred around births" (p. 5), defining the family as "a partnership between a man and a woman with common children" (p. 8), and rejects "the preferential treatment of a gender to overcome actual or perceived discrimination" (FPÖ 2011, p. 8). The Spanish radical right party Vox aims to eliminate "all gender legislation," including quotas, and instead promote policies enhancing the stability of families (Vox 2023, p. 10). In Germany, the radical right Alternative for Germany commits itself to the traditional family model as a "guiding principle" and aims to increase birth rates, among others by "opposing all attempts to trivialize abortion, to promote it on the part of the state, or to declare it a human right" (AfD 2016).

The aforementioned examples show how rising political authoritarianism and restrictive women's and LGBTQI+ rights legislation seem to go hand in hand at the level of political elites, resulting in the dismantlement of democratic institutions and human rights, even in established liberal democracies that are relatively advanced economically. However, we know little about how attitudes toward gender equality (GE), freedom of sexuality (FS) and political authoritarianism are related at the individual level and across countries.

On the individual level, the psychological literature on authoritarianism has either considered GEFS values as part of a large battery of questions measuring authoritarianism without theorizing the distinct role of GEFS values in developing authoritarian attitudes (e.g., Adorno et al. 1950, Altemeyer 1983), or, the literature considers authoritarianism a predictor of sexism rather than a consequence of individuals' GEFS values (e.g., Sibley, Wilson and Duckitt 2007). On the country level, the most relevant literature focuses on populations' attitudes toward GEFS as fundamental to measuring parts of a larger emancipative value system and considers the role of this broader value system in driving democratic values and achievements across countries (e.g., Welzel 2013). Yet, this approach has largely neglected what is distinct about these attitudes from the perspective of gender and gender socialization that uniquely impacts the development of individuals' attitudes toward political authoritarianism. Finally, a few studies working within the emancipative values framework find that FS attitudes are particularly important in enabling individuals and democratic countries to withstand illiberal challenges (Alexander and Welzel 2017; Welzel, Kruse and Brunkert 2022). However, these studies do not develop a theory of how individuals' and populations' FS attitudes are related to opposition to political authoritarianism, in particular. This has led to criticism that these studies lack the support of more nuanced theory and analysis of how these attitudes impact regime support (Foa, Mounk and Klassen 2022).

Overall, the theory and evidence on the relationship between emancipative gender values and attitudes toward authoritarian political leadership is underdeveloped. We begin to fill this gap by engaging with two questions in this Element. First, to what extent do people's gender and sexuality values influence their support of an authoritarian leader? And, second, at the societal level, to what extent are gender and sexuality norms related to mass attitudes toward political authoritarianism? In engaging with these questions, we focus, first, on the individual level and theorize how and why individuals' GEFS values are important predictors of their attitudes toward political authoritarianism. On this front, we argue that individuals begin developing GEFS values through gender socialization early, during childhood, in the family and in the more local, community forms of education and norm socialization to which they are exposed. In addition, these values continue to develop by being reinforced or challenged as individuals become adults, select the communities they participate in and decide how gender will structure their intimate and personal relationships in their households. Given that gender structures are fundamental to how individuals develop in and embed over their lifecycles in their most significant social relations, these structures carry the normative capacity to influence how individuals understand and conform to other systems of social relations. On this front, as we will develop, we note that progressive GEFS values are incompatible with political authoritarianism because this is a system rooted in and sustained through conformity to hegemonic masculine dominance and progressive GEFS values clash with conformity to that dominance. We argue that progressive GEFS values exert a direct negative effect on individuals' support for political authoritarianism through socializing this rejection of conformity to hegemonic masculine dominance. We also argue that progressive GEFS values further buttress individuals' opposition to political authoritarianism indirectly through strengthening support for pluralism, strengthening support for democratic socialization in households, and increasing rejection of the use of violence to control social relations in households. Through these direct and indirect processes, the development of an individual's GEFS values influence the formation of their attitudes toward political authoritarianism.

Having established how and why we would expect individuals' GEFS values to influence their attitudes toward political authoritarianism, we then turn to the country level and consider how GEFS norms and political authoritarian norms are related as mutually reinforcing cultural processes as countries experience shifts in these norms over time. On one front, we theorize that increasingly progressive GEFS norms among the population increase the population's opposition to political authoritarianism for reasons that align with our individual-level expectations. On the other front, we theorize how increases or decreases in political authoritarian culture potentially influence GEFS norms. Thus, at the country level, we expect a mutually reinforcing relationship between these two sets of norms over time as countries develop culturally.

We use World Value Survey (WVS) data from 1995 to 2022 (waves 3–7) of all available OECD countries to test these arguments at the individual and the aggregate country level (individual level: $n = 70,000+$ in max. 26 countries; country level: $n = $ max. 74 in max. 28 countries, varying by model specification).[1] We limit our sample to OECD countries to ensure we include relatively advanced and globalized economies that, to some extent, commit to shared standards and values in terms of "individual liberty, democracy, the rule of law, human rights, gender equality, environmental sustainability and tackling inequalities" (OECD 2024, p. 3). In economic and political terms, these societies should offer conditions for developing emancipative values, including GE and FS values. Further, in these contexts, support for political authoritarianism is more clearly associated with a scenario of democratic backsliding. Political authoritarianism is not the status quo; rather, the status quo is some tradition of stable democratic institutions. This ensures comparability in the meanings respondents associate with political authoritarian leadership relative to democracy across the sample of countries we analyze. Finally, choosing OECD countries allows us to include countries from several world regions, including Latin America, Asia, and Western countries, to ensure our findings are not specific to Western countries.

We apply multilevel ordered logistic regression analysis to test the relationship between GEFS values and political authoritarian attitudes at the individual level. We further apply mediation analysis using structural equation modeling to

---

[1] See Online Appendix I for list of available countries and survey waves.

investigate different mechanisms through which GEFS values and political authoritarian attitudes are related at the individual level. At the aggregate country level, we apply seemingly unrelated regression and panel regression analyses to model the mutually reinforcing dynamics between GEFS norms and political authoritarian norms.

Our findings suggest that progressive GEFS values at the individual level are indeed predictors of political anti-authoritarian attitudes, and this relationship is partly mediated by (a) pluralist attitudes, (b) democratic values regarding childhood socialization, and (c) opposition to the use of violence to control social relations in households. At the country level, our analysis generates results consistent with the theory of a mutually reinforcing relationship between GEFS norms and political authoritarian norms, which is particularly driven by the relationship between FS norms and political authoritarian norms.

Taken together, the Element's theoretical and empirical work on both the individual and country levels offers comprehensive, new insights into the relationship between individuals' GEFS values and their attitudes toward political authoritarianism and the interaction between a society's GEFS norms and its political authoritarian norms. Moreover, these findings carry important implications for the real world, demonstrating that a progressive GEFS socialization can constitute a potential tool for building and maintaining resilience to the formation of political authoritarian attitudes in individuals. Conversely, a conservative GEFS socialization likely fosters the formation of political authoritarian attitudes and increases the acceptance of political authoritarian leadership among individuals. At the country level, our findings demonstrate the importance of safeguarding hitherto achieved advances in women's and LGBTQI+ rights, policies and educational awareness in developed democracies, given the recent rise of authoritarian leaning leaders and radical right parties that contribute to an increasingly authoritarian political culture and potentially threaten these advances through the accompanying mobilization of normative opposition to GEFS.

The Element is structured as follows. Section 1 introduces previous research and theory that we build on in developing our argument on the relationship between GEFS and political authoritarianism at the individual level. In Section 2, we present our data and methodology, as well as our empirical analysis on the individual level. Section 3 presents previous research and theory that we build on in developing our argument on the relationship between GEFS and political authoritarianism at the country level. Section 4 then presents the data, methodology, and empirical analysis at the aggregate country level. Finally, Section 5 concludes with a discussion of our main findings, suggestions for future research, and a discussion of the implications of our Element for the current political situation in developed democracies.

1 A Theory of Individuals' GEFS Values and Their Attitudes toward Political Authoritarianism

In this Element, we focus on the concept of political authoritarianism developed largely by comparative political scientists as forms of political leadership that do not subject leaders to accountability by the individuals they lead through core democratic mechanisms of periodic, free elections. By using this definition of political authoritarianism, we take a rather conservative and minimalist stance on this concept. In fact, authoritarian measures, including the removal of checks and balances on the government or the restriction of civil liberties, can be implemented by freely elected political leaders. In other words, a political leader may be elected in free elections and still be considered authoritarian or authoritarian-leaning. By defining political authoritarianism as support for political leadership that does not subject to the accountability mechanism of periodic, free elections, we aim to ensure that our definition is as unambiguous as possible: Clearly, support for this type of political leadership can be considered support for political authoritarianism.

Working off this conceptualization of political authoritarianism, we are particularly interested in understanding the variation in support for this type of leadership among electorates of more developed democracies through public opinion research. In this pursuit, we join the amassing recent scholarship that, as Merkel and Lührmann (2021, p. 869) note, commonly observe "that the main contemporary challenge to democracy is its gradual demise after illiberal or authoritarian-leaning political leaders come to power in elections and aggrandize their prerogatives at the cost of parliaments and independent judiciaries."

Adding to this body of recent work, and in light of the various attacks by political leaders on women's and LGBTQI+ advances that we observe in recent years, we develop a theory of the distinctive role played by emancipative gender values in the development of opposition to political authoritarianism. Building on research on emancipative value change (Inglehart and Norris 2003; Alexander and Welzel 2011; Welzel 2013), we understand emancipative gender values as expressed by individuals' attitudes toward GEFS. GE values, in the way that we conceptualize them in this Element, regard the acceptance of equal suitability and opportunity for women and men in the public sphere, namely in universities, the labor market and politics. We conceptualize FS values as freedom of sexual orientation, support of the right to divorce and support of abortion rights.[2] Working with these conceptualizations of GE and FS, we theorize the role of GEFS values in shaping individuals' opposition to political authoritarianism in this section.

---

[2] This conceptualization is conditioned by the available data on aspects of freedom of sexuality. Ideally, we would have liked to include attitudes toward trans rights and/or gender fluidity. However, such data is not available.

1.1 Disentangling Authoritarianism and GEFS Values

To examine how GEFS values relate to the tendency for individuals to oppose authoritarian-leaning political leaders it is necessary to disentangle authoritarianism and GEFS values. Thus, we depart from the established tradition of research that measures a broader category of authoritarian attitudes to understand and identify "authoritarian followers." This is a tradition that builds from the pivotal work of Adorno et al. (1950) and continues to approach the question of authoritarian support with studies that work largely with the broader measures of authoritarianism captured by Altemeyer's (1983; 2007) Right-Wing Authoritarianism (RWA) scale and Pratto et al.'s (1994) Social Dominance Orientation (SDO) scale. The RWA scale is composed of items based on survey questions that measure a range of different attitudes on deference to authorities, gender roles, sexuality, religion, and social conservativism. The SDO scale relies on several survey questions to measure individuals' attitudes toward unequal relations among social groups.

Given our focus of inquiry, a fundamental problem with the RWA scale's measure of authoritarianism is that the measure conflates individuals' lack of GEFS values with support of authoritarianism. Several of the RWA scale items ask respondents about their attitudes toward GE and FS. Given the aim of this Element and as we develop in our theoretical work next, we see GEFS values as playing a distinct and fundamental role in the development of opposition to authoritarianism, political authoritarianism in particular. In contrast to previous work using the RWA scale, we therefore conceptualize and measure political authoritarianism as an attitude that is distinct from, but related to, individuals' GEFS values.

When it comes to the SDO scale and its focus on attitudes toward unequal relations among social groups, while groups such as men, women or LGBTQI+ are not asked about explicitly, the general focus of the items on group inequalities risks considerable conceptual overlap with attitudes toward these groups, which GEFS captures. Thus, using the SDO scale to conceptualize and measure political authoritarianism would create problems with conceptual overlaps that our focus on the minimalist notion of political authoritarianism avoids.

In line with the literatures on RWA and SDO, another strand of literature conceptualizes authoritarianism as the valuing of order and sameness in society and has measured authoritarianism via items that capture the importance ascribed to child qualities such as good manners and obedience, or the lack of importance ascribed to child qualities such as tolerance and respect for other people (Stenner 2005; Engelhardt, Feldman and Hetherington 2023). The valuing of order and sameness, indeed, captures intolerance for challenges to traditional norms and structures, including GE and FS, among others. Thus, similar to RWA and SDO, this conceptualization of authoritarianism is closely related to GEFS and creates similar problems for our aim to understand the distinctive role of GEFS values in shaping opposition to political authoritarianism among individuals.

Given that our aim is to focus on authoritarianism in the political sphere and investigate its relationship with GEFS values, we thus conceptualize political authoritarianism as support for political leadership that does not subject leaders to the accountability mechanism of periodic, free elections. The concept of support for political authoritarianism on which we focus is more minimalist than the previously described broader measures in its limit to attitudes toward political leaders based on their defiance of core democratic institutions. The focus on political authoritarianism in terms of its institutional characteristics enables us to disentangle political authoritarianism from GEFS values and explore the relationship between them, rather than merging them into one concept. Thus, while our minimal focus on political authoritarianism is ultimately motivated by our aim to contribute a gender perspective to the overall understanding of the current authoritarian challenges to democracy, we also consider our minimalist focus advantageous compared to broader conceptualizations of authoritarianism in our efforts to understand the distinctive role of GEFS values in shaping opposition to political authoritarianism among individuals.

Having acknowledged this departure from the broader literature in our conceptualization and subsequent measurement of authoritarianism, we nevertheless build on and engage with research that has attempted to understand the drivers and implications of support for authoritarianism through the broader RWA and SDO approaches to the concept, as well as through childrearing values. Indeed, the first part of the section reviews the literature on the relationship between attitudes and values related to GEFS and these broader measures of authoritarianism among individuals and then develops the Element's theory of how individuals' development of GEFS values distinctly affects their opposition to political authoritarianism. The theory development also draws support from this larger literature on authoritarianism in addition to work on gender structures and hegemonic masculinity. Finally, it develops our argument that GE and FS values are closely related yet differ from each other at the individual level.

1.2 Why Individuals' GEFS Value Formation Is Distinct from and Influential of Their Attitudes toward Political Authoritarianism

From its beginning, attitudinal research attempting to measure and understand variation in individuals' authoritarian tendencies has considered their GE and FS attitudes central. Questions on aspects of FS were used to measure some of the traits Adorno et al. (1950) theorized as constituting the authoritarian personality syndrome. In addition, some of the statements used to measure authoritarianism with the RWA scale cover some aspect of GE or FS (Altemeyer 2007). These approaches suggest that individuals' GE and FS belief constructs and their experiences with gender and sexuality that led to the development of those constructs are profoundly related to whether they accept authoritarianism. Accordingly, several studies examine relationships between authoritarian attitudes and individuals' GE and FS beliefs through the broader approaches of the RWA and SDO scales.

Several studies have observed relationships between RWA and traditional gender beliefs (Duncan, Peterson and Winter 1997; Duncan 2006; Peterson and Zurbriggen 2010), as well as relationships between RWA, SDO and sexist attitudes (Russell and Trigg 2004; Sibley, Wilson and Duckitt 2007; Christopher and Wojda 2008; Akrami, Ekehammer and Yang-Wallentin 2011; Christopher, Zabel and Miller 2013; Austin and Jackson 2019). Moreover, several studies have observed relationships between RWA, SDO, and attitudes related to FS, such as those focused on reproductive rights (Duncan, Peterson and Winter 1997; Peterson and Zurbriggen 2010) and LGBTQI+ attitudes (Chamorro Coneo, Navarro, and Quiroz Molinares 2022). Studies have also measured authoritarianism through childrearing values and, similar to the literature working with the measures of RWA and SDO, find a relationship between authoritarian childrearing values and rejection of sexual minorities (Oyamot et al. 2017) and transgender rights (Miller et al. 2017). Thus, a rather robust link between broader measures of authoritarian attitudes and various measures of GE and FS attitudes among individuals is supported by a large body of empirical work. However, as outlined earlier, these studies come with the shortcoming that the measurements of authoritarianism are not clearly distinct from GEFS attitudes.

Further, contrary to the theory we develop next, throughout these studies, individuals' authoritarian attitudes, broadly conceived, are presented and interpreted as explaining individuals' lack of GE and FS values; the measures of RWA and SDO are predominantly presented as independent variables and the measures of GE and FS attitudes as dependent variables. Hence, the implied direction of influence is that individuals develop authoritarian belief systems that come prior to and influence their GE and FS beliefs. Our work departs from this by proposing a theory that supports the opposite direction of influence. We offer a theoretical framework for understanding how GEFS values influence political authoritarian attitudes.

Accordingly, in this Element, we develop the argument that individuals experience gender and sexuality and develop gender and sexuality beliefs that influence their attitudes toward political authoritarianism. We return to the work of Altemeyer (1983, 2007) and relate this to work on the socializing influence of gender and sexuality structures to build this argument. Altemeyer argues that authoritarian beliefs are a product of social learning; these beliefs are learned and developed through interactions with household and community agents of socialization that characterize the stable and consequential primary environments in which individuals develop from infancy into young adulthood. These beliefs are learned and developed through social interactions with, for instance, parents, peers, religious institutions, schools, and the media. Research suggests that one of the earliest, if not the earliest, ways individuals are exposed in their development to more or less authoritarian relations is through systems that structure gender and sexuality in their households and communities (Stockard 2006; Ridgeway 2009). People who are embedded in families and communities marked by more patriarchal and heteronormative gender and sexuality structures are exposed to manifestations of authoritarian relations which potentially shape their leadership ideals and their likelihood to oppose or support political authoritarianism.[3]

How do these structures socialize individuals to be more accepting of authoritarian leadership? In their more exaggerated forms, patriarchal and heteronormative gender and sexuality structures socialize individuals embedded in those structures to be more accepting of authoritarian leadership by developing values for social conformity to hegemonic masculinity. Hegemonic masculinity is here understood as a "practice that permits men's collective dominance over women to continue" (Connell and Messerschmidt 2005, p. 840). This can, but does not necessarily, include toxic practices and violence aimed at stabilizing "gender dominance" (Connell and Messerschmidt 2005, p. 840). Hegemonic masculinity is sustained by policing men to conform with it, as well as excluding and discrediting women in exercising dominance (Connell and Messerschmidt 2005, p. 841). Importantly, the concept recognizes that multiple masculinities exist within a hierarchy of masculinities and individuals' personalities are complex such that most men do not live up to hegemonic masculinity (Connell and Messerschmidt 2005, p. 846). Thus, rather than understanding hegemonic masculinity as embodied by individual men, it is understood as a constructed system of authority based on an

---

[3] We want to emphasize here that we do not argue that individuals who are embedded in more patriarchal and heteronormative structures over their development are *always* more accepting of political authoritarianism. We are not endorsing that deterministic logic here as we recognize the complexity and diversity of structures individuals potentially engage with throughout their development and their capacity to have agency over those structures. We instead work with a probabilistic logic here and assume, based on our theory, that the more individuals are embedded in those structures over their development the more likely it is that this will directly and indirectly increase their support of political authoritarianism.

ideal of masculinity and a model of gender relations (Connell and Messerschmidt 2005, p. 838). This model of gender relations manifests in various ways, including through discursive practices (Connell and Messerschmidt 2005, p. 841), cultural consent, "institutionalization, and the marginalization and delegitimization of alternatives" (Connell and Messerschmidt 2005, p. 846). As such, hegemonic masculinity can also be upheld by complicit men who do not live up to it but still receive the benefits of patriarchy (Connell and Messerschmidt 2005, p. 832), as well as conforming women and women who appropriate parts of hegemonic masculinity for their own benefit, for instance to enable a successful career (Connell and Messerschmidt 2005, p. 847).

Conformity to hegemonic masculinity manifests in norms and institutions through which ultimate authority in households and communities is monopolized by heterosexual men and maintained through hierarchical heterosexual male networks. That hegemonic masculine monopoly of authority manifests in the relegation of women to subservient roles and the discrimination against women that limits their ability to acquire resources and power. Moreover, one of the primary ways order and camaraderie are maintained among men in these systems is through patriarchal norms and institutions that control female sexuality, buttressing the importance and the value of heterosexual relations. Patriarchal and heteronormative gender and sexuality structures allow men to unite and respect one another through mutual recognition of their right to exploit and control women and the children they make with those women. One of many consequences of these structures is therefore that homosexuality is considered unacceptable for maintaining social order. Thus, these structures are repressive of both GE and FS in order to preserve the hegemonic masculine monopoly of authority.

In addition, the practice of hegemonic masculinity is exemplified by forceful, potentially violent forms of authority (Manne 2017). In its most extreme form, it justifies the exertion of violence to control and police women, children and men who break with the system to maintain order in the household and corresponding communities (Manne 2017). Finally, the system of logic that justifies conformity to hegemonic masculinity is ultimately based either on religion (Seguino 2011) – "it is the word of God" – or some set of alleged laws of nature (Hyde et al. 2019). Such alleged laws of nature include the ideas that males are naturally superior to females, female biology renders females naturally inferior or at least different from males in ways that make females unsuitable for leading roles in society, and homosexuality is unnatural. Importantly, whether the logic behind these structures is justified by religion or "nature-based" laws, it is dogmatic, nondeliberative, and absolute. Thus, social order under patriarchal and heteronormative gender and sexuality structures is ultimately maintained through socializing individuals' conformity to strong, potentially violent, uncontested hegemonic masculine leadership. As we argue next, political authoritarianism is rooted in and sustained by hegemonic masculine dominance and conformity to that dominance.

To the contrary, more progressive GEFS structures expose individuals to more diversity in who makes household and community decisions, who occupies which social roles, and how identities are expressed (Ridgeway 2009). Under these structures, individuals' most personal, intimate, and primary social relations are governed by a greater emphasis on personal choice and equality of opportunity to develop capabilities and influence over decision-making. As a result, a plurality of ways of self-expressing, behaving, role assuming, and aspiring become possible for individuals because these freedoms are less restricted by rigid societal assumptions about them based on how their gender is perceived. Thus, those who are more embedded in more progressive household and community GEFS structures over their lifecycles are more likely to develop diversity and personal autonomy values that are rooted in how these individuals experience diversity in gender and sexuality relations. Meanwhile, those who are more embedded in patriarchal and heteronormative gender and sexuality structures over their lifecycles are more likely to develop values for social conformity to hegemonic masculinity.

As mentioned earlier, we argue that political authoritarianism is rooted in and sustained by hegemonic masculine dominance and conformity to that dominance. Political authoritarian leaders and political authoritarian-leaning leaders in democracies are and have historically predominantly been heterosexual men, prone to strong, violent, and uncontested leadership. Even in the cases of women and gay authoritarian-leaning leaders in democracies, these leaders symbolize, practice, and, ultimately, conform to hegemonic masculinity by making misogyny and homophobia a part of their political agendas (Kaul 2021; Chenoweth and Marks 2022). In addition, women authoritarian-leaning leaders tend to explicitly embody traditional stereotypes of women as mothers and carers in their own behavior (Meret 2015; Geva 2020). Given the hegemonic masculine nature of political authoritarianism, it is therefore likely that the gender and sexuality structures in which individuals are embedded from childhood through early adulthood influence their opposition to or support for political authoritarianism. As described earlier, the degree to which these structures are more conservative or progressive in terms of GEFS fundamentally affects whether individuals are subjected to authoritarian relations marked by conformity to hegemonic masculine dominance or relations that structure gender and sexuality according to personal autonomy and tolerance. In turn, these gender and sexuality structures that characterize the individuals' families and communities shape individuals' leadership ideals which then shape individuals' opposition to or support for political authoritarianism.[4]

1.3 Why GE and FS Are Not Necessarily the Same

So far, we have treated GEFS values as a combined set of closely related values regarding gender equality and freedom of sexuality. In the following, we will argue that GE and FS values differ in important ways.

Our main argument here is that FS values remain much more contested than GE values in contemporary societies. As we noted earlier, GE values, in the way that we conceptualize them in this Element, regard the acceptance of the equal suitability and opportunity of women and men in the public sphere, namely in universities, the labor market and politics. While these places have traditionally been highly dominated by men and partly remain so, women and men are equally likely to go to university in many societies today. Further, especially when required by the economic situation of the household, many women

---

[4] The idea that individuals develop ideals through exposure to household relations, such as parenting, that they then draw on to reason politically is also supported by Lakoff's (1996) *Moral Politics Theory*. This theory develops the argument that individuals rely on their understanding of family relations in developing ideas of how society should function. The concrete relations that individuals experience in their family environments generate an ideal moral system of social relations that guide individuals' larger, more abstract moral belief systems about how society should function. Moral Politics Theory posits two worldviews that derive from individuals' family relations and consequent ideals: the strict model and the nurturant model. These models involve the development of beliefs about ideal traits in children and ideal parenting derived from exposure to individuals' own household relations. Under the strict model, the disciplining of children to be nonindulgent, self-reliant and capable in an inherently competitive and dangerous world is emphasized through more strict hierarchical relations and deference to the primary authority in the family, typically the male head of household. Under the nurturant model, the fostering of an inherently good nature in children is emphasized through developing their empathy, tolerance, cooperation and empowerment for the purposes of social cooperation and social responsibility. The nurturant model thus derives from family relations structured according to transparent and openly discussed rules that adhere to the principles of empathy, openness, accountability and respect for others. These differing systems of assumed child traits and ideal family relations generate differing moral systems for individuals that they then use for reasoning over the more abstract social and political functions of society. In particular, the strict and the nurturant models structure and form differences in individuals' tendency to adhere to conservative or progressive values in reasoning over the social and political functions of society. Recent experimental work has generated robust evidence consistent with this theory (Barker and Tinnick 2006; Feinberg and Wehling 2018). Our theoretical assumptions overlap with those of Lakoff's Moral Politics Theory in the focus on how the structures of social relations characterizing the families and communities in which individuals grow up shape ideals that they eventually draw on in their political reasoning. However, we focus, in particular, on how *the gender and sexuality structures* characterizing the individuals' families and communities *shape individuals' leadership ideals* which then *shape individuals' opposition to or support for political authoritarianism*. In the absence of longitudinal, panel data on the individual-level, we however refrain from analyzing the lifecycle argument implied in Lakoff's theory on how childhood experiences influence the later development of political values.

engage in paid work, even though they are less likely than men to work full-time and take up leading business positions, and the gender pay gap persists in almost all contemporary societies. Finally, while politics are still male-dominated in many societies and women in politics face a particular type of violence (Krook 2020), gender quotas are increasingly common in politics and women increasingly hold high political offices in various countries. While men may still play a relatively minor role in taking care of the household and the family in most societies, women have come to play a more important role in many societies' public spheres.

Thus, a larger percentage of people, particularly those of younger generations, may be socialized in a family where, for instance, both the father and the mother attended university, or both the father and the mother engage in paid work to some extent. We thus expect more people to hold relatively progressive GE values compared to their FS values.

Moreover, FS values remain more contested in many societies. In this Element, given the data that is available to us, we conceptualize FS values as freedom of sexual orientation, support for the right to divorce, and support for abortion rights. In contrast to the earlier conceptualization of GE values, these values challenge men's position of authority in the private sphere, including the family and the home. Where the norms of heterosexuality and male dominance are challenged and women have the right to divorce and have an abortion, men lose their patriarchal control over the women and children in their family. In contrast to the previously described normalization of women's participation in the public sphere, FS values are less normalized. In particular, sexual orientation and abortion remain highly contested issues in some developed democracies. In fact, laws securing the rights to abortion and LGBTQI+ rights are among the latest ones to be implemented and the first ones to be attacked by conservatives in several contemporary Western societies, including recently in Poland, Hungary, and the United States. Despite the European Union's strong commitments to protect and promote human rights, even its Member State Malta has one of the strictest anti-abortion laws in the world, and Ireland only legalized abortion in 2018. As regards LGBTQI+ rights, same-sex marriage is still not legalized in various European Union countries at the time of writing. Worldwide in 2020, only eleven countries protected the right to same-sex sexual acts by constitutional law, while thirty countries punished such acts with long prison sentences or even the death penalty.[5]

As FS values remain contested, we expect people to differ more strongly in their FS values than in their GE values. In fact, while we expect GE and FS

---

[5] https://ilga.org/maps-sexual-orientation-laws.

values to go somewhat hand in hand given their common roots in the progressive transformation of the traditional system of heterosexual male dominance, we also expect that some people with relatively progressive GE values may hold relatively more conservative FS values. This is because, as we have argued, challenging male authority over the family still remains more contested in contemporary democracies than women's participation in the public sphere.

1.4 A Theory of GEFS and Opposition to Political Authoritarianism in a Nutshell

Based on the earlier discussion, overall, we expect that individuals with stronger GEFS values are less likely to support political authoritarianism due to the incompatibility of their value system with social conformity to hegemonic masculine dominance. In addition to this, we also expect that through the development of stronger GEFS values, individuals develop (1) a more general value for pluralism; (2) a more general value for democratic socialization in households; and, (3) an aversion to the use of violence to control social relations in households. In turn, we expect that through a more general value for pluralism and democratic socialization in households, and an aversion to the use of violence to control social relations in households, the strength of individuals' GEFS values will further reduce their support for political authoritarianism.

On the *pluralism* pathway, political authoritarianism functions through the support of conformity and sameness over autonomy and pluralism. Patriarchal and heteronormative gender structures profoundly socialize conformity and sameness. They repress the diverse ways that individuals can potentially express and relate through emphasis on conformity to rigid self-presentations, behaviors, roles and ambitions based on one's perceived gender. In addition, this conformity is legitimated by dogmatic, nondeliberative appeals to "laws of god or nature" (Seguino 2011; Hyde et al. 2019). Thus, the utility of pluralism in expressing, behaving, and organizing in individuals' most personal and intimate social contexts is limited under these structures. On the contrary, under progressive GEFS structures a plurality of ways of self-expressing, behaving, role assuming and aspiring are possible for individuals, because these freedoms are not restricted by rigid societal assumptions about them based on how their gender is perceived. Under these conditions, pluralism in expressing, behaving, and organizing in individuals' most personal and intimate social contexts is useful in establishing meaningful relationships and a value for pluralism generally is socialized.

On the *democratic socialization in households* pathway, political authoritarianism functions through resistance to democratizing social relations generally.

A primary way that social relations are practiced more democratically or authoritatively in individuals' private and intimate lives is in their households (Miklikowska and Hurme 2011). Under patriarchal and heteronormative gender structures, social relations in the household are governed by hegemonic masculine dominance. Under this dominance, conformity and obedience in social relations are valued and this, in turn, potentially increases the valuing of political authoritarianism as a way of governing social relations outside the household. On the contrary, under progressive GEFS structures, social relations in the household are more open and expressive and rules and boundaries more negotiable. In this context, tolerance and deliberation as opposed to obedience in social relations are valued, and this, in turn, potentially increases the valuing of democratic ways of governing social relations outside the household, hence challenging political authoritarianism.

Finally, on the *aversion to household violence* pathway, political authoritarianism functions through the uncontested, hegemonic masculine monopolization of violence by the state. Acceptance of this monopolization and use of violence can partly be developed through exposure to and conformity to the uncontested, male-dominant monopolization of violence by the traditional, male head of household and the use of this violence to control social relations within the family. Violence by a male head of household is more common in households with patriarchal and heteronormative gender structures (Lomazzi 2023). On the contrary, under progressive GEFS structures, there are lower levels of intimate partner violence and violence used on children for disciplinary purposes (Baniamin 2022).

Moving ahead with the empirical test of this theory, in the next section, we assess the direct and indirect relationships between individuals' GE and FS values and their attitudes toward political authoritarianism. We investigate these relationships separately for GE and FS values because GE and FS constitute different ways of transforming traditional heterosexual male dominance and societies are generally more progressed in GE than in FS.

2 An Analysis of How Individuals' Support of GE and FS Decreases Their Support of Political Authoritarianism

Having outlined the literature and theory underlying our argument that progressive GEFS values are related to political anti-authoritarianism at the individual level, this section proceeds to test this argument empirically. Based on the earlier theoretical framework, we also test to what extent these variables' relationship is mediated by (a) pluralist attitudes, (b) democratic values regarding childhood socialization, and (c) opposition to violence to control social relations in households.

2.1 The Strategy for Testing Our Theoretical Arguments

We work with data on roughly 70,000+ individuals from 28 OECD countries based on waves 3–7 of the World Values Surveys (Inglehart et al. 2020).[6] By constraining our sample to OECD countries, we aim to ensure a certain (albeit limited) comparability in terms of the countries' development of democratic and economic institutions over the studied time period from 1995 to 2022. Given their rather advanced economic and political development, these societies should offer conditions for developing emancipative values, including GE and FS values. At the same time, the OECD countries comprise societies marked by different gender cultures, including, for example, Turkey, South Korea, Mexico, and Sweden, which provides us with interesting variation on one of our main variables. The variation in political authoritarianism at the country level is rather limited, in comparison. Because authoritarianism is not the status quo in these contexts, strong political leadership should evoke comparable associations among respondents, where support for political authoritarianism is associated with a scenario of democratic backsliding. Still, the OECD countries comprise countries with varied authoritarian past and present regimes and experiences with democratic backsliding, including for instance Turkey, and countries with a rather recent authoritarian past, such as Southern European and post-Communist countries. We thus hope that constraining our sample to OECD countries ensures a reasonable level of comparability in terms of economic and institutional development while providing us with interesting variation in our main variables. Finally, choosing OECD countries enables us to include countries from several world regions, including Latin America, Asia, and Western countries, to ensure our findings are not specific to Western countries. However, given limited data availability, we do not claim that our findings are representative for all OECD countries.

2.1.1 Our Main Variables of Interest: GEFS Values and Political Authoritarian Attitudes

At the individual level, we distinguish between gender equality indicators and freedom of sexuality indicators, which we summarize in two separate indexes ranging from 0 to 1 where higher values equal higher support for gender equality and freedom of sexuality.[7] The gender equality index comprises three survey indicators (Cronbach's alpha: 0.6837), for each of which respondents are asked to indicate their agreement or disagreement on scales ranging from 1 to 3, or 1 to 4:

---

[6] See Online Appendix I for a full list of countries.
[7] In so doing, we follow others working with the same WVS data in political culture research (see, for instance, Inglehart and Norris 2003; Welzel 2013).

(1) When jobs are scarce, men should have more right to a job than women (1–3 scale)

This indicator aims at capturing respondents' attitudes about gender roles in the labor market. It should tap into whether men are regarded as the main breadwinners whose responsibility as providers for a family comes first and prevails over women's ambitions to pursue a career. We expect that respondents who agree with this statement consider women's labor force participation or career ambitions as secondary to men's jobs and careers. More implicitly, given that men and women often build a family together which entails a lot of care work, prioritizing men's careers also entails an endorsement of women's role as primarily the main caretakers. Beyond the literal meaning of the survey indicator, agreement with this indicator can therefore be interpreted as endorsement of traditional gender roles regarding the division of labor in the household.

(2) A university education is more important for a boy than for a girl (1–4 scale)

While university education is equally accessible to young men and women by law, traditional social norms may discourage young women from pursuing a university education and encourage (or even pressure) young men to do so. Similar to the previously described indicator, this indicator taps into the idea that men's role is to pursue a successful career and potentially be able to financially provide for a family, while women's professional careers are of lower importance.

(3) On the whole, men make better political leaders than women do (1–4 scale)

This indicator captures ideas about both gender roles and gender stereotypes. Agreement with the statement that men make better political leaders entails, first, an endorsement of traditional gender roles, in which men take power over public offices and political decision-making and women are concerned with the family and household, that is, the private sphere. Second, agreement with this statement may imply agreement with stereotypical ideas about men's and women's supposed nature: Traditional gender stereotypes often imply that certain leadership qualities such as assertiveness, vigorousness, competitiveness, knowledgeability, ambition, effectiveness or objectivity are associated with masculinity (Ryan et al. 2011, Aaldering and Van der Pas 2020). Conversely, women are stereotyped as gentle, empathetic, compassionate, emotional, altruistic, weaker, and caring for other people, which may partly contribute to empathetic leadership but tends to be associated with a lack of those leadership qualities that are stereotyped as masculine (Aaldering and Van der Pas 2020). Agreement with the statement that men make better political leaders may thus imply both agreement with traditional gender roles and with stereotypical ideas about the supposed nature of men and women.

In addition to a gender equality index comprising the three previously described indicators, we build a freedom of sexuality index to capture another set of respondents' gender values.[8] Rather than capturing respondents' values about men's and women's roles in society and their agreement with gender stereotypes, the freedom of sexuality index captures respondents' attitudes toward aspects of sexual self-determination. Like the gender equality index, the freedom of sexuality index ranges from 0 to 1 and comprises three indicators (Cronbach's alpha: 0.8035). Specifically, respondents are asked to indicate *to what extent they consider it justifiable to (1) have an abortion, (2) have a divorce, and (3) be homosexual*. Herein, the response scale ranges from 1 (never justifiable) to 10 (always justifiable).

It is noteworthy that the first two indicators ask about potential choices that can depend on the affected person's circumstances, that is, the choices to have an abortion or a divorce. In contrast, the third indicator asks about homosexuality, which is not a choice and does not depend on individual circumstances. In addition, the first indicator is clearly gendered: Only biological women can have an abortion. Conversely, divorce and homosexuality are not explicitly gendered, as all genders can have a divorce or be homosexual. While the three indicators of the freedom of sexuality index are thus not entirely comparable, they all capture different aspects of sexual self-determination that challenge the idea of the traditional heteronormative nuclear family including heterosexual marriage and children. They thus help us understand to what extent respondents are accepting of such freedom of sexuality.

Different from the previously described gender equality indicators that capture attitudes toward norms about gender roles and stereotypes in society, the freedom of sexuality indicators are concerned with attitudes toward what is justifiable behavior in terms of abortion, divorce, and homosexuality. In some of the studied countries and time periods, rights protecting the justifiability of these behaviors, particularly abortion and homosexuality, are politicized and contested, and some of the studied countries do not grant these rights or do so only to a limited extent. However, many of the studied countries have also been granting the rights to abortion, divorce, and homosexuality for decades. We therefore expect a rather high variation in public support for the justifiability of these behaviors. Unfortunately, the available data does not allow us to capture support for more recently evolving debates in the realm of sexual and gender self-determination laws, such as the debates about transgender people's rights.

---

[8] In so doing, we follow others working with the same WVS data in political culture research (see, for instance, Inglehart and Norris 2003; Welzel 2013).

While the previously described GEFS measures constitute our independent variables, the dependent variable aims to capture political authoritarian attitudes. As we covered extensively in our review of the relevant literature, authoritarianism is usually measured by large survey batteries including indicators about authoritarianism in various life spheres. In contrast, we explicitly focus on authoritarianism in relation to a country's political system. By doing so, we aim to isolate political authoritarianism from authoritarianism in other life spheres, such as in the household or in social group relationships. Isolating political authoritarianism has at least two advantages. First, it enables us to study the relationship between political authoritarianism and gender values in isolation of each other without conflating the two. Second, it captures a kind of authoritarianism that is directly related to a country's democratic institutions, enabling us to make an argument about implications for people's attitudes toward democracy and their countries' democratic culture.

We understand political authoritarianism as the notion of a strong political leader who faces little checks and balances and cannot be held accountable by the people. The indicator we use to capture this concept asks respondents to rate different types of political systems on a 1-to-4 scale, where 1 equals "very good" and 4 equals "very bad." The type of political system we use to capture respondents' attitudes toward political authoritarianism reads as follows: *Having a strong leader who does not have to bother with parliament and elections.* We thus consider people who find this type of political system "very good" (1) as politically authoritarian, and people who find it "very bad" (4) as politically anti-authoritarian. A key advantage of this measure is that it uses concise and tangible language, describing a form of political authoritarianism without using abstract, loaded terms such as "authoritarianism" or "democracy." Research shows that people who express support for democracy ascribe different meanings, and even partly authoritarian meanings, to the term "democracy" (Kirsch and Welzel 2019). While support for democracy is widespread, the meaning of support for democracy differs widely across contexts. In contrast to broader measures of support for democracy or authoritarianism, the wording of the measure used in this Element ensures that respondents understand the measure in tangible and comparable ways.

Having described the measures of our independent and dependent variables, Figures 1 and 2 show the distributions of our two independent variables: the gender equality index and the freedom of sexuality index. As expected, the figures illustrate that freedom of sexuality is the more contested indicator, compared to gender equality. While most people in the studied sample tend to reveal rather gender equal attitudes about gender roles and gender stereotypes, overall, there clearly is more opposition to sexual self-determination in the form of having an abortion or a divorce or being homosexual.

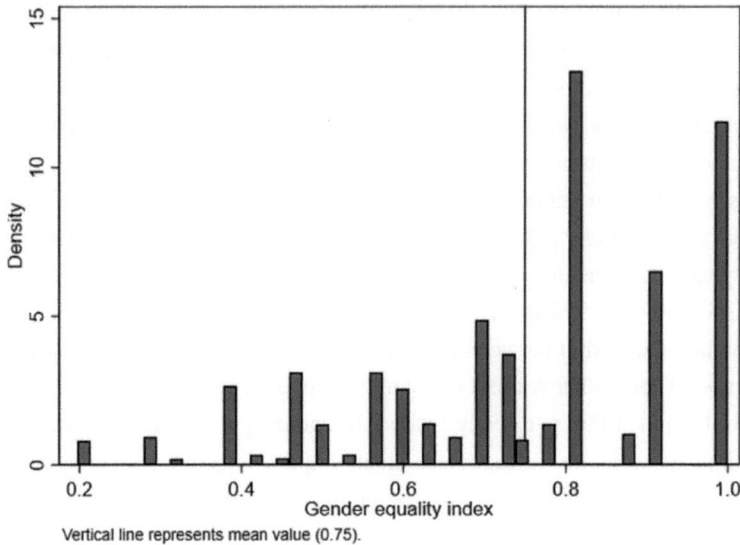

Figure 1 Distribution of the gender equality index

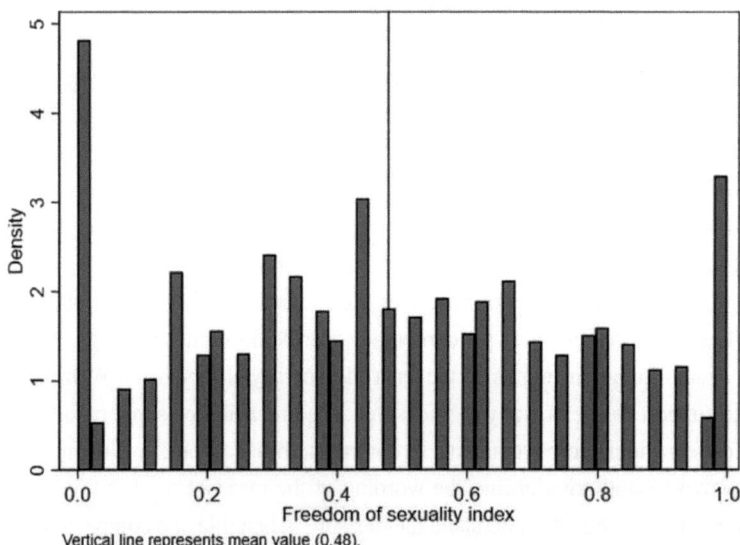

Figure 2 Distribution of the freedom of sexuality index

As regards our dependent variable, that is, attitudes toward strong (unchecked) political leadership, Figure 3 shows that, while most respondents consider strong leadership as "very bad" or "bad," there is a considerable number of respondents (33.2 percent) considering strong leadership as "good" or "very good." The data thus provides us with interesting variation in GEFS values and attitudes toward

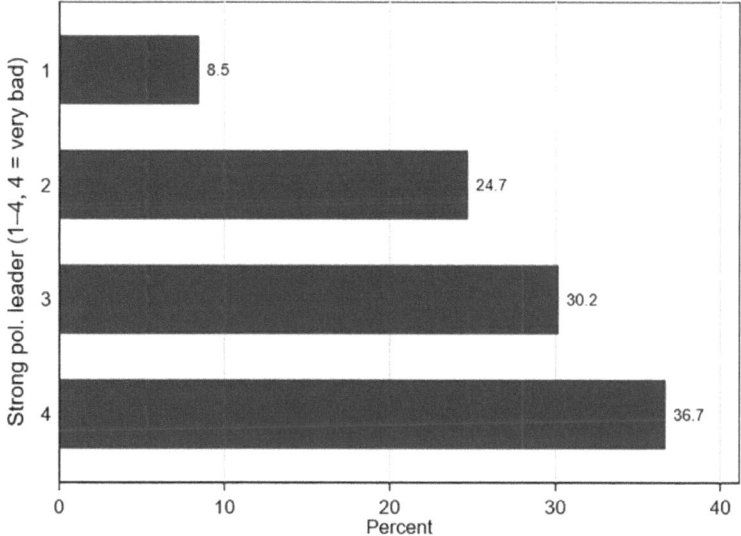

Figure 3 Distribution of political authoritarianism

political authoritarianism to explore within the context of OECD countries over the past quarter-century.

2.1.2 How GEFS Attitudes and Political Authoritarianism Relate to Each Other

To illustrate how GEFS attitudes and political authoritarianism are related to each other, Figure 4 shows respondents' mean authoritarian attitudes over their GEFS values, pooling the full sample of respondents from all survey waves and countries. For both GEFS indicators, the tendency is similar: Respondents with more progressive GEFS values are more anti-authoritarian, and vice versa. This is in line with the theoretical argument that progressive GEFS values are related to political anti-authoritarianism at the individual level.

To better understand the variation in these variables over time and across cohorts, Figures 5–7 show the mean values of these variables by birth cohort and survey wave. Overall, the figures show a trend of younger respondents revealing less authoritarian and more progressive GEFS attitudes. This is especially the case for attitudes toward freedom of sexuality: The contested nature of this indicator partly plays out between the older and the younger generations. In addition to younger generations being more progressive, the graphs show that respondents of the earlier survey waves 3 and 4 (1995–2004) tend to hold less progressive GEFS attitudes/values than respondents of survey waves 5–7 (2005–2022). Again, this is particularly the case for freedom of

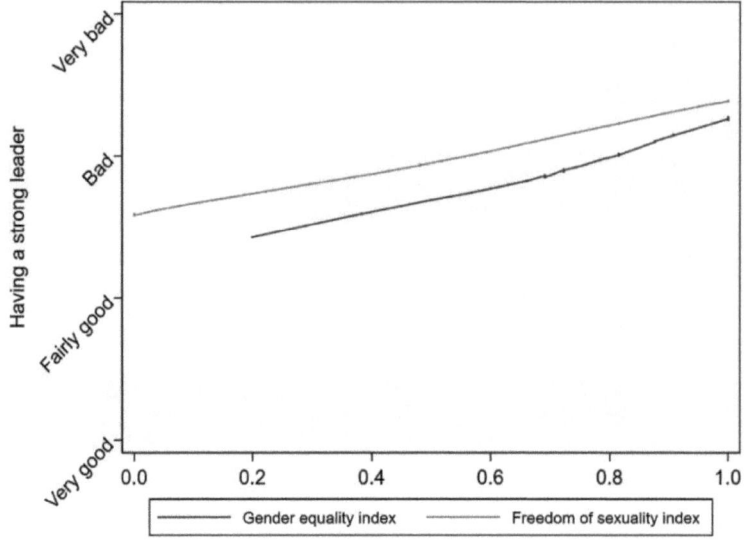

Figure 4 Mean political anti-authoritarianism over gender equality and freedom of sexuality values

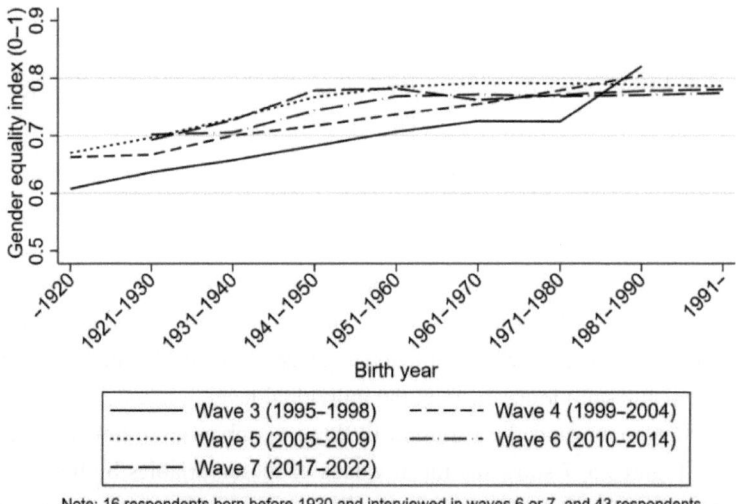

Figure 5 Gender equality index development across generations and over time

sexuality attitudes. This pattern illustrates that respondents of the same birth cohorts become more supportive of freedom of sexuality over time. Figure 6 shows that this effect is particularly pronounced for respondents born between 1941 and 1960, a generation often described as the *Baby Boomers*.

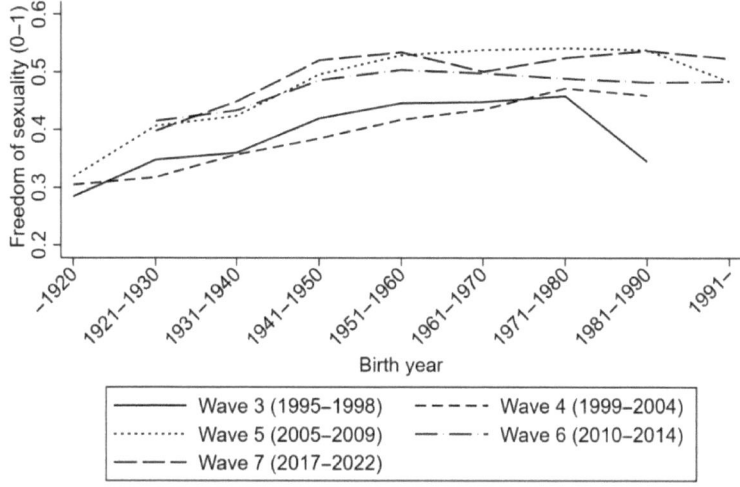

Figure 6 Freedom of sexuality index development across generations and over time

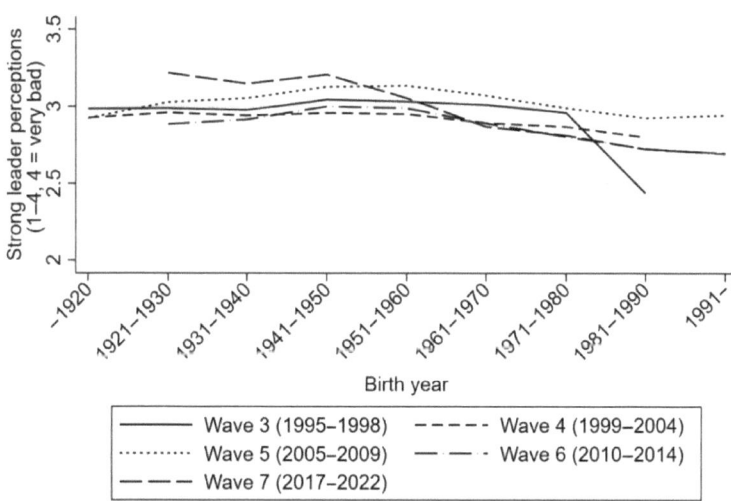

Figure 7 Political authoritarianism across generations and over time

As regards authoritarian attitudes (Figure 7), the development over time is less clear. For instance, older respondents of wave 3 (1995–1998) are nearly indistinguishable in their mean authoritarian attitudes by birth cohort from older respondents of wave 6 (2010–2014). Respondents of wave 4 (1999–2004) of all birth cohorts hold slightly more authoritarian values than others, perhaps pointing to a period effect – a big change that occurs at a particular point in time and increases all generations likelihood to become more supportive of a strong and unchecked political leader. In our sample, respondents of wave 7 (2017–2022) that were born before 1950, as well as respondents of wave 5 (2005–2009) that were born after 1960 hold the least authoritarian attitudes. Overall, Figure 7 shows rather unclear patterns as to the development in people's attitudes toward political authoritarianism. This may reflect the fact that the past quarter-century has observed both democratizing and autocratizing trends within and across countries, as well as instances in which strong, unchecked political leadership was temporarily demanded, for instance in response to terrorist attacks.

2.1.3 Digging Deeper into the Relationship between GEFS Values and Political Authoritarianism

As we investigate the relationship between the gender equality index, the freedom of sexuality index and our measure of political authoritarianism, we are further interested in three mediating variables that we expect to channel part of the relationship between respondents' gender values and political authoritarianism: (1) support for pluralism, (2) support for democratic socialization in households and (3) opposition to the use of violence in households to control social relations. In other words, we expect that respondents' gender values affect their attitudes toward pluralism, democratic household socialization, and domestic violence, which in turn should affect their attitudes toward political authoritarianism. By exploring these relationships, we aim at better understanding through which mechanisms GEFS values affect political authoritarianism.

Support for Pluralism

We measure support for pluralism by respondents' support for freedom of speech. Respondents are asked to prioritize between four political measures: Maintaining order in the nation, giving people more say in important government decisions, fighting rising prices, and protecting freedom of speech. We consider those respondents who give first or second priority to the protection of freedom of speech as supportive of pluralism. Freedom of speech is a fundamental prerequisite to allow for pluralism of political opinions in a society, as it allows people to speak freely without pressure to conform to politically. Sartori (1997) describes the central characteristic of the pluralistic worldview using the term "dissent" – meaning freely differing in opinion, which is essentially enabled by freedom of speech. We expect that progressive GEFS values are positively related to support for pluralism, given that a divergence from traditional gender and sexuality norms leads to an

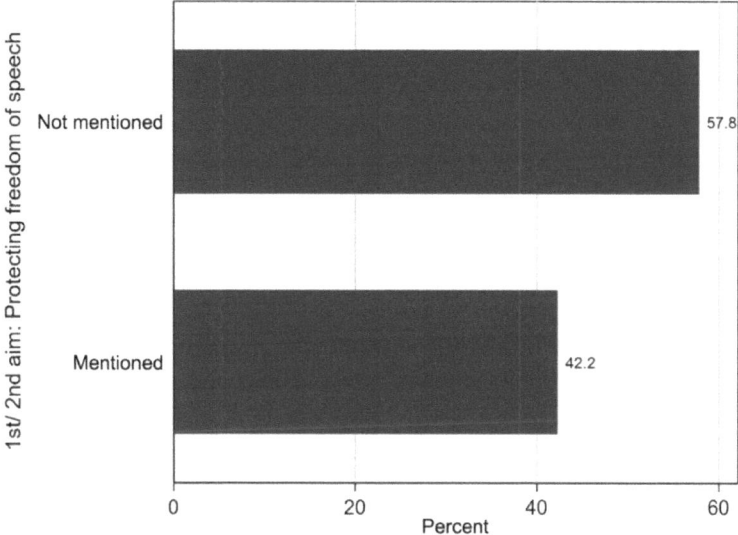

Figure 8 Support for pluralism (operationalized by giving priority to freedom of speech)

increased plurality in how gender and sexuality are expressed and practiced in society. People who support nontraditional expressions of gender and sexuality should thus be more likely to endorse pluralism in society in general.

We further expect that a support for pluralism, in turn, is related to less endorsement of political authoritarianism, since political authoritarianism by nature is anti-pluralist, oppressive of political opponents and minorities. In fact, Sartori (1997) argues that "pluralism is inimical to majority rule," if majority rule is understood in the "literal and strong sense of the term" rather than as a consensus that the majority should respect minority rights (p. 63). Support for pluralism may thus partially mediate the relationship between GEFS values and political authoritarianism. Figure 8 shows the distribution of our measure of support for pluralism, that is, whether respondents mention freedom of speech as their first or second priority for their countries when given four items to choose from. In our full sample, 42.2 percent of respondents mention freedom of speech as their first or second priority and are thus considered as supportive of pluralism.

Support for Democratic Socialization in Households

In addition to support for pluralism, we expect that support for democratic socialization in households channels part of the relationship between GEFS values and political authoritarianism. Individuals that hold progressive GEFS values are open to more diverse and deliberative ways of organizing households, because they rely less on gender as a way to structure expectations, roles, and decision-making. In this context, tolerance and deliberation in social relations are valued, and this, in turn, potentially increases democratic socialization in the household. One way to capture the value for democratic socialization in households is by measuring individuals' support for anti-authoritarian attitudes toward childhood socialization. Researchers have examined this through questions on the priority individuals give to tolerance over obedience as child qualities (Stenner 2005; Engelhardt, Feldman and Hetherington 2023). Thus, in terms of their values about childhood socialization, people with progressive GEFS values should value tolerance, while obedience should not be particularly important to them.

To measure these attitudes toward childhood socialization, we rely on an indicator asking respondents to indicate a maximum of five out of ten listed qualities that children can be encouraged to learn at home, asking which qualities the respondent considers especially important. Among others, the listed qualities include "tolerance and respect for other people" and "obedience." We use this information to construct a measure of anti-authoritarian attitudes toward childhood socialization ranging from 0 to 2, where 2 equals most anti-authoritarian values. Respondents who indicate tolerance *and* do not indicate obedience as important qualities score the highest (coded as 2). Respondents who *either* mention *both* tolerance and obedience *or* do not mention *any* of these qualities are coded as 1.[9] Finally, respondents who *do not* mention tolerance and *do* mention obedience score lowest and are thus considered as most authoritarian (coded as 0) with regard to their attitudes toward childhood socialization.

We expect that (anti-)authoritarian attitudes toward childhood socialization should in turn affect how people view their countries' political systems. People who do not value tolerance and consider obedience an important childhood quality should be more likely to endorse similar values with regard to politics. In other words, they should be more likely to favor a strong political leader who does not have to bother with parliament and elections, that is, a leader who does not have to bother with tolerating the political representation and expression of minorities, including people who deviate from prevalent gender and sexuality norms, and a leader who can enforce conformity (obedience) with their leadership without being subject to checks and balances. Figure 9 shows the

---

[9] The middle category of the democratic household socialization variable includes people who indicated both "tolerance and respect for other people" and "obedience" as important qualities, as well as people who indicated neither of these qualities as important. Because these people may systematically differ from each other, we include robustness checks running two more analyses: One analysis excluding people who indicated both "tolerance and respect for other people" and "obedience" as important qualities, and one analysis excluding people who indicated neither of these qualities as important. The results are shown in Online Appendix Tables A17–A20. The results hold and remain significant ($p<0.01$), but the mediation effects are slightly smaller in all robustness checks.

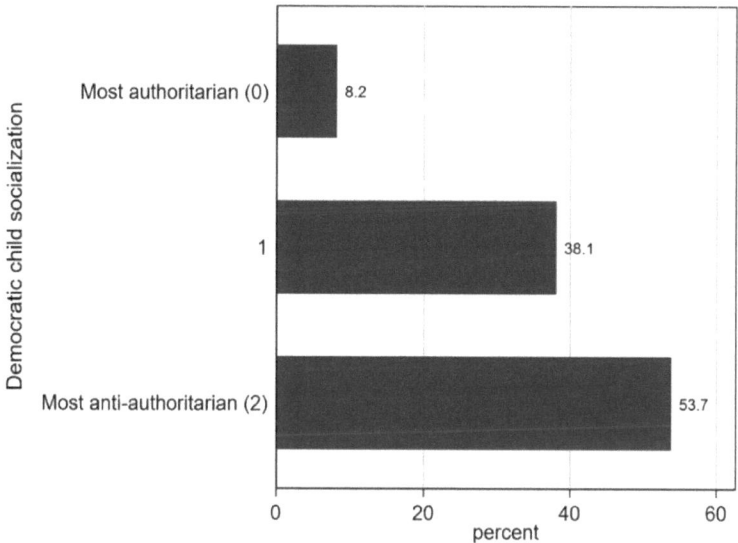

Figure 9 Democratic household socialization operationalized by anti-authoritarian attitudes toward childhood socialization

distribution of anti-authoritarian attitudes toward childhood socialization in our sample, where 53.7 percent are considered as most anti-authoritarian and 8.2 percent are most authoritarian with regard to their attitudes toward childhood socialization.

Opposition to the Use of Violence to Control Household Social Relations

Third and finally, we expect that opposition to violence in the household channels part of the relationship between GEFS values and political authoritarianism. People who endorse traditional gender roles, in which men hold power positions in society, should be more likely to believe in men's superiority and women's and children's inferiority in the household as well. Of course, this does not necessarily imply an endorsement of violence. However, a man's sense of entitlement to his position in the household and women's compliance with this expectation sets the basis for a man to take action and enforce women's and children's compliance, and, in the worst case, use physical domestic gender-based violence and violence on children to do so (Manne 2017; Baniamin 2022; Lomazzi 2023). Moreover, under conformity to more rigid structures of hierarchy in the household to control household relations, people who endorse more traditional gender roles may also consider it acceptable for both parents to discipline their children with physical violence given that children occupy the most inferior position in the household hierarchy.

People who tend to justify domestic violence, including hierarchical relationships in the household and the use of force to uphold these hierarchies should, in turn, be more likely to endorse such hierarchies in a political system as well. In other words, they should be more likely to hold political authoritarian attitudes by endorsing strong political leadership that monopolizes violence by the state and has the capacity to use that violence to enforce decisions unchecked.

To measure the extent to which people justify domestic violence, we use two survey indicators asking to what extent respondents consider it justifiable (1) for a man to beat his wife, and (2) for parents to beat their children. Respondents are asked to answer on a scale from 1 to 10, where 1 equals "never justifiable" and 10 equals "always justifiable." Because domestic violence is generally condemned in many societies, it is socially desirable for respondents to answer that both types of domestic violence are never justifiable, and indeed, our data show that most respondents answer that way. However, as we know that domestic violence occurs in all societies,[10] we suspect that all respondents who do not indicate that domestic violence is "never justifiable"; that is, all respondents who indicate a higher value than 1 on the scale from 1 to 10, to some extent endorse domestic violence. Given that the only socially acceptable answer option would be to indicate that domestic violence is never justifiable, any respondent who indicates that domestic violence is to some extent justifiable cannot be considered as entirely opposing of domestic violence.

Thus, to construct a measure capturing the opposition to domestic violence, we build a measure ranging from 0 to 2, where higher values equal stronger opposition to domestic violence. Respondents who indicate that it is never justifiable for a man to beat his wife and for parents to beat their children are coded as 2. Respondents who consider only one of these forms of domestic violence as never justifiable are coded as 1. Finally, respondents who indicate that neither of these forms of domestic violence is never justifiable are coded as 0, and thus least opposed to domestic violence according to our measure.

It is noteworthy that the survey indicators capturing opposition to domestic violence are only available in the World Value Survey's survey waves 6 and 7, capturing the time period from 2010 to 2022. We thus constrain this part of our analysis to these survey waves. Constraining the analysis to survey waves 6 and 7 results in a sample of 37,826 observations from 17 countries. While this reduces our sample considerably, the sample still provides a wide geographical scope, comprising countries from North America, Latin America, Oceania, East Asia, the Middle East (Turkey), and East and West Europe. Figure 10 shows the distribution of our measure of opposition to domestic violence in our sample,

---

[10] www.unwomen.org/en/what-we-do/ending-violence-against-women/facts-and-figures.

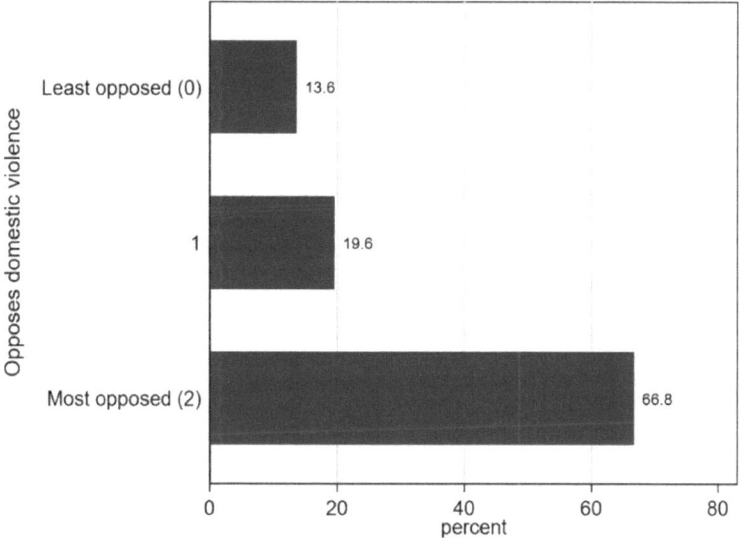

Figure 10 Opposition to domestic violence

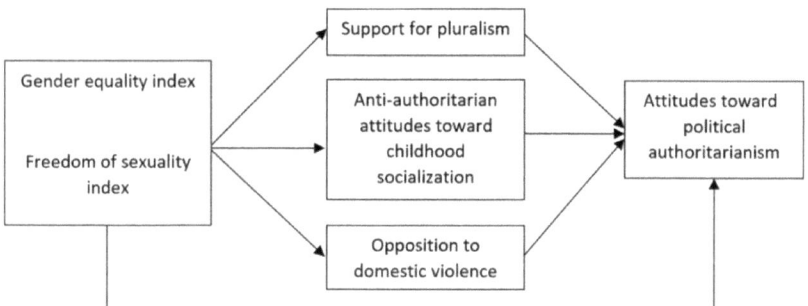

Figure 11 A summary of the main investigated relationships at the individual level

where 66.8 percent are most opposed and 13.6 percent are least opposed to domestic violence.[11]

Overall, Figure 11 visually summarizes the main explored relationships between our independent variables (the gender equality index and the freedom of sexuality index) and the dependent variable measuring attitudes toward

---

[11] Domestic violence between partners is a highly gendered phenomenon, given that most domestic violence between partners is exerted by men toward women. In fact, the wording of the survey indicator we use explicitly suggests that men beat their wives. Given the explicitly gendered nature of the indicator and the generally gendered nature of domestic violence in society, we conduct the analysis of the relationship between GEFS values, opposition to domestic violence, and political authoritarianism separately for men and women in Online Appendix II.

political authoritarianism, and the three mediating variables: Support for pluralism, anti-authoritarian attitudes toward childhood socialization, and opposition to domestic violence. In the following, to test our theoretical expectations, we proceed to investigate each of the displayed relationships separately.

2.2 What the Data Show

To empirically confirm the theorized distinction between gender equality and freedom of sexuality at the individual level, we begin by performing an unrotated principal component analysis (PCA) on the 6 GEFS indicators. In so doing, we include the available data from all OECD countries and WVS waves 3–7 and standardize all indicators (Inglehart et al. 2020).

The PCA confirms that two Eigenvalues are greater than 1, indicating that two components explain more variance in the data than accounted for by one variable in the original standardized dataset. Figure 12 shows how the different gender equality and freedom of sexuality indicators load on the two identified components. In Figure 12, it appears clearly that the three freedom of sexuality indicators, that is, "Justifiable: abortion," "Justifiable: divorce," and "Justifiable: homosexuality," load on Component 1 with loadings ranging from 0.4344 to 0.4666 (see the x-axis). Conversely, the three gender equality indicators load on Component 2 with loadings ranging from 0.3354 to 0.4924 (see the y-axis). These indicators are "When jobs are scarce, men should have more right to a job than

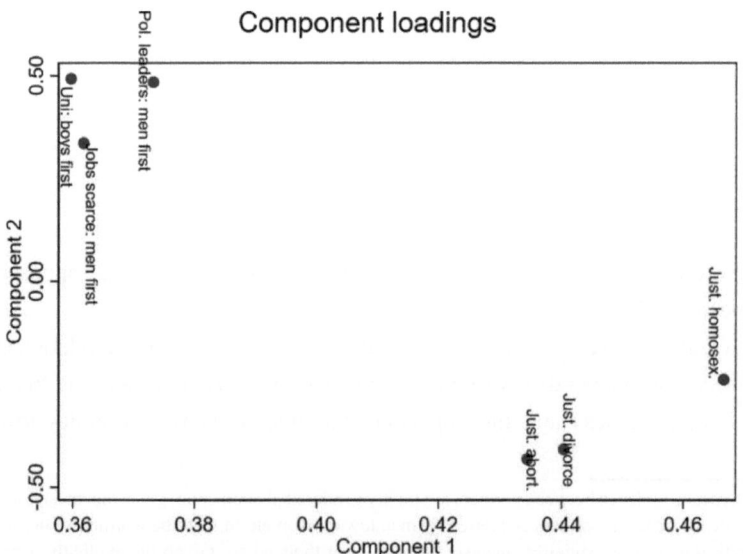

Figure 12 Loading plot: How the GE and FS indicators load on the two identified components

women," "A university education is more important for a boy than for a girl," and "On the whole, men make better political leaders than women do." The PCA thus empirically confirms our theorized distinction between gender equality and freedom of sexuality indicators. In the following, we proceed with our analysis with two separate independent variables: the gender equality index and the freedom of sexuality index.

To empirically substantiate our argument on the relationship between political authoritarianism and GEFS values, we run a multilevel ordered logistic regression analysis of authoritarian attitudes on gender equality and freedom of sexuality attitudes, allowing for random intercepts at the country level, and controlling for proxies of authoritarianism and variables that are known to be related to authoritarianism and GEFS values at the individual level. Theoretically, the nature of our data of individuals nested in countries justifies the choice of multilevel modeling. Empirically, the Intraclass Correlation Coefficient (ICC) of 0.13 indicates that 13 percent of the variation in authoritarian attitudes is explained at the country level, confirming the adequacy of multilevel modeling. Multilevel modeling accounts for the variation of authoritarian attitudes explained at the country level, allowing us to analyze within-country variation in authoritarian attitudes between different individuals, which is the focus of this part of our analysis. Given the limited availability of the used survey indicators, this model is run on data from WVS survey waves 6–7 only.

Our control variables include survey indicators capturing whether respondents consider the following two features as essential characteristics of democracy: people obeying their rulers and civil rights. We further control for whether respondents consider democracy as important, whether they consider violence against other people as justifiable and whether they consider respect for authorities as good or bad.

Theoretically, these variables should be closely related to political authoritarianism: People who favor a strong political leader who does not have to bother with elections and parliament should be more likely to favor people obeying their rulers (Mallinas, Crawford and Frimer 2020). In contrast, they should favor social order over individual freedoms (Feldman 2003) and thus be less likely to consider civil rights as important. Similarly, political authoritarian people should be more likely to consider state violence (Eckhardt 1991), and, thus, under certain circumstances, violence against other people as justifiable, and generally more likely to value respect for authorities (Mallinas, Crawford and Frimer 2020). In contrast to some evidence suggesting that people in authoritarian regimes express support for democracy because they ascribe more authoritarian meanings to the term "democracy" (Kirsch and Welzel 2019), we expect that political authoritarian people in our sample are *less* likely to consider democracy as important. This is because we expect people in our sample of (relatively developed) democracies to have some basic knowledge of the institutions of electoral democracy, including elections and a parliament, which are explicitly at odds with our measure of political authoritarianism. Controlling for these variables thus serves to control for a range of theoretically strong predictors of political authoritarianism. As we theoretically elaborate earlier, these variables may also be related to GEFS values as they tap into different aspects of (political) authoritarianism: Given the hierarchical and partly oppressive nature of traditional gender roles and the conformist nature of rejecting freedom of sexuality, GEFS values should be related to these control variables.

We further control for respondents' nationalist attitudes, left–right ideological self-identification, level of education, the importance they ascribe to God as a measure of religiosity, subjective assessment of their income level, age, and gender. Given that (radical) right-wing nativist parties have been identified as a risk factor for democratic backsliding (Norris 2017) and voters take cues from their favored political parties (Leeper and Slothuus 2014), we expect nativism and right-wing ideology to be positively related to political authoritarianism. The exclusive and hierarchical nature of nativist ideology toward immigrants and ethnic minorities (Mudde 2007) further parallels the exclusive and hierarchical nature of authoritarian politics toward political minorities and opponents, leading to potential overlaps between the two ideologies. We control for respondents' level of education because higher education tends to be associated with more liberalism (Lindskog and Oskarson 2022), which should lead to more progressive GEFS values and less support for political authoritarianism. Conversely, religiosity tends to be related to more traditional values, norm conformity, and greater respect for authorities (Pless, Tromp, and Houtman 2021). In line with research showing that threat perceptions can activate authoritarian predispositions (Feldman and Stenner 1997) and given the fact that economic precarity and instability can evoke threat perceptions, we expect that people with lower income can be more supportive of political authoritarianism. Finally, we expect older generations to be more supportive of political authoritarianism (Norris and Inglehart 2019).

Figure 13 shows the results of multilevel ordered logistic regression analysis. Progressive gender equality and freedom of sexuality values each are strong predictors of political anti-authoritarianism. For a full-range increase from 0 to 1 on the gender equality index, the odds of finding strong political leadership "very bad" are 2.57 times higher than the combined odds of finding strong political leadership very good, fairly good or bad. Similarly, progressive freedom of sexuality values are related to political anti-authoritarianism, albeit to

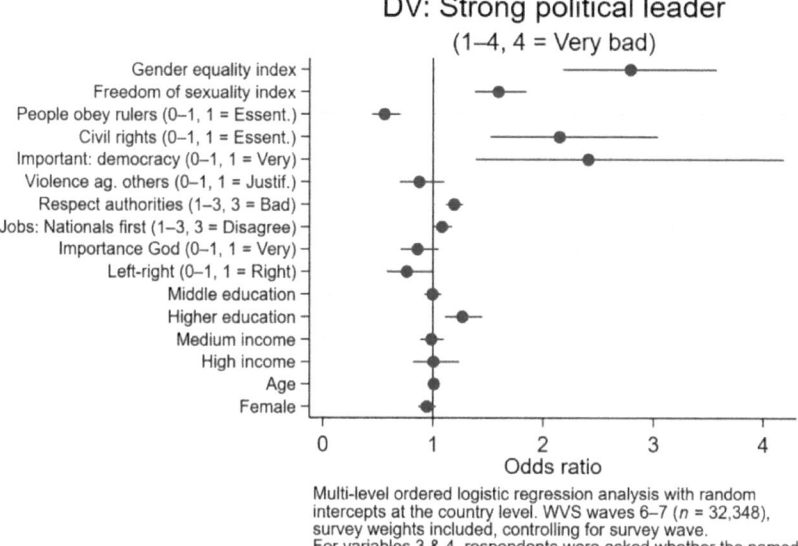

Figure 13 The relationship between political (anti-)authoritarianism and GEFS values

a smaller extent. For a full-range increase from 0 to 1 on the freedom of sexuality index, the odds of finding strong political leadership "very bad" are 1.52 times higher than the combined odds of finding strong political leadership very good, fairly good or bad. The effects of gender equality and freedom of sexuality values on political anti-authoritarianism are thus significant, both in terms of statistical significance and in magnitude, even when controlling for other important predictors of political (anti-)authoritarianism.

Our control variables either show the expected relationships with political authoritarianism, or no significant relationship. Considering obedience an essential aspect of democracy is related to more support for political authoritarianism, while regarding civil rights as essential for democracy is related to less support for political authoritarianism. Similarly, finding democracy important, considering respect for authorities as bad, and upper education are related to less support for political authoritarianism. Right-wing ideology is related to more support for political authoritarianism, and disagreement with nationalism is related to less political authoritarianism. However, when controlling for all aforementioned variables, there is no significant relationship between support for political authoritarianism and justifying violence against other people, religiosity, income, age, and gender.

The results quite strikingly support our expectations that gender equality and freedom of sexuality values are strongly related to political anti-authoritarianism, even when controlling for a range of strong predictors of authoritarian attitudes. Traditional values regarding gender roles and gender stereotypes, as well as sexual self-determination beyond traditional heteronormativity seem to be essential in explaining support for authoritarian political leadership with large effect sizes compared to other important predictors. It is noteworthy that the relationship between gender equality attitudes and political authoritarian attitudes is stronger than the relationship between freedom of sexuality attitudes and political authoritarian attitudes. One potential explanation for this difference may be related to the different natures of the gender equality and the freedom of sexuality indicators. The gender equality indicators tap into attitudes about the acceptability of men's superiority over women in different spheres of society. Thus, these indicators rather closely measure conformity to hegemonic masculinity, which we theorize is a system in which political authoritarianism is rooted and through which political authoritarianism is sustained. In contrast, the freedom of sexuality indicators tap into whether respondents find behaviors that defy conformity to hegemonic masculine dominance as justifiable, but they do not tap into the acceptance of the superiority of traditional heterosexual masculinity over other expressions of gender identity. In this case, these indicators do not directly capture conformity to hegemonic masculine dominance from a freedom of sexuality perspective.

Finally, to attain a better understanding of how gender equality and freedom of sexuality values are related to political authoritarianism and to explore the mechanisms behind this relationship, we use structural equation modeling to conduct a mediation analysis. Based on the previously described theoretical framework, we test the mediating effects of (1) support for pluralism, (2) anti-authoritarian values regarding childhood socialization, and (3) opposition to domestic violence.

Baron and Kenny (1986), often cited as one of the first articles to delineate a systematic approach to mediation analysis, test mediation in three steps: First, the independent variable needs to predict the dependent variable. Second, the independent variable needs to predict the mediating variable, and third, the independent variable and the mediating variable together need to predict the dependent variable. While these conditions can be tested by means of regression analysis, later work has established the use of structural equation modeling (SEM) to conduct mediation analyses (Iacobucci et al. 2007). The advantage of SEM consists of the fact that the models are estimated simultaneously while statistically controlling for the respective other. We thus run SEM followed by the Sobel's z-test and the Monte Carlo test to test for mediation based on the SEM results.

As Imai, Keele, and Tingley (2010) point out, a drawback of SEM is that it assumes linear relationships between continuous variables. However, our dependent variable capturing political authoritarianism, as well as two mediator variables are categorical, and one mediator is binary, thus violating the SEM assumption. A solution would be to run a generalized SEM (GSEM) instead, which can account for the variables' types. However, it would not allow running relevant post-estimation mediation tests. We thus adopt the following strategy: We start by running a GSEM specifying the correct functional forms of the models. Second, we run an SEM and compare its results with GSEM results. Responding to the criticism by Imai, Keele and Tingley (2010), we further run a mediation analysis using the *medeff* command as a robustness check (Hicks and Tingley 2011), which allows for binary and continuous, however not categorical mediators or outcome variables. As the results are highly similar, we continue to run the post-estimation mediation tests on the SEM results.

While SEM allows us to include multiple mediators simultaneously, we choose to run separate estimations for each mediator to not overcomplicate the models.[12,13] For all analyses, we use standard errors clustered at the country-level to account for the structure of the data. Further, we control for standard socioeconomic and demographic variables likely to affect our variables of interest: age, gender, education, importance of God (religiosity), and WVS wave dummies (waves 5–7) in all models. All models apply survey weights.

According to Imai, Keele and Tingly (2010), for a mediation analysis to identify causal pathways, the sequential ignorability assumption must hold. In our analysis, this assumption does not hold: We cannot convincingly argue that freedom of sexuality and gender equality values are independent of all mediators and of anti-authoritarian attitudes, and all mediators are independent of anti-authoritarian values. Further, while we control for age, gender, education,

---

[12] Correlations between the three mediators are as follows. Pluralism and democratic child socialization: 0.083 (*p*-value: 0.000); pluralism and opposition to domestic violence: 0.032 (*p*-value: 0.000); democratic child socialization and opposition to domestic violence: 0.1067 (*p*-value: 0.000).

[13] While we run separate analyses for each mediator in our main analyses, we add robustness checks to the Online Appendix (Online Appendix II, 8, Tables A21–A22, Figures A1–A2), in which we jointly consider all mediators in the same analysis. We do so to account for the fact that the mediators are significantly correlated with each other, even though the correlations are small in magnitude. The robustness check largely confirms the mediation effects that are found to be significant in the main analysis. However, in contrast to what we find in the separate analysis of mediators, the mediation effect of anti-authoritarian child socialization (M) on the relationship between the freedom of sexuality index (X) and anti-authoritarian values (Y) is only significant at the 90 percent significance level when studying all mediators jointly.

religiosity, and survey wave, and while we cluster standard errors at the country level, we cannot rule out that there are unobserved pre- and posttreatment confounders. Therefore, we do not treat these mediation analyses as causal. Rather, we are interested in analyzing the likely interplay between the analyzed variables, and particularly, the likely pathways through which gender equality and freedom of sexuality values relate to anti-authoritarian values, without necessarily identifying causal pathways.

Figure 14 shows the path diagram visualizing the mediation effects tested for the first independent variable, that is, the gender equality index. Herein, the parameters a, b, and c' denote regression coefficients. The direct effect of the gender equality index (X) on strong leader perceptions (Y) is denoted as c', while the indirect effect of X on Y that is mediated through one of the mediators (M) can be quantified as a*b. Calculating the percentage of the total effect (c' + (a*b)) that is explained by the indirect effect (a*b) will determine the mediation effect. As previously mentioned, the models are run separately for each mediator for simplicity reasons.

For the first independent variable, that is, the gender equality index, we find significant mediation effects for all mediators. First, support for pluralism (i.e., prioritizing the protection of freedom of speech) mediates 6.8 percent of the effect of the gender equality index on strong leader perceptions (see Figure 15).[14] In other words, 6.8 percent of the relationship between the gender equality index and strong leader perceptions is explained by the fact that people with progressive gender equality values tend to hold more pluralist attitudes, which in turn is related to their more anti-authoritarian attitudes.

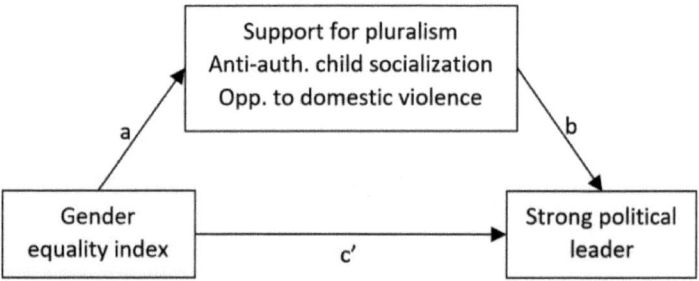

Figure 14 Hypothesized mediation effects for the relationship between gender equality values and authoritarianism

Note: *All models control for gender, age, education, importance of God (religiosity), and survey wave (excluded from visualizations for visibility purposes). Survey weights are included; standard errors are clustered by country. The sample comprises WVS waves 3–7 of OECD countries. For the third mediator, that is, opposition to domestic violence, we have data for waves 6–7 only.*

---

[14] Robustness check using *medeff* command: 5.9 percent mediation effect.

Attitudes toward Political Authoritarianism

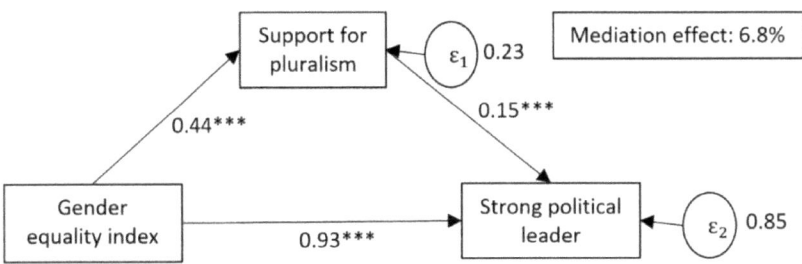

Figure 15 SEM results. Independent variable: gender equality index; mediator: support for pluralism. *** = $p < 0.001$

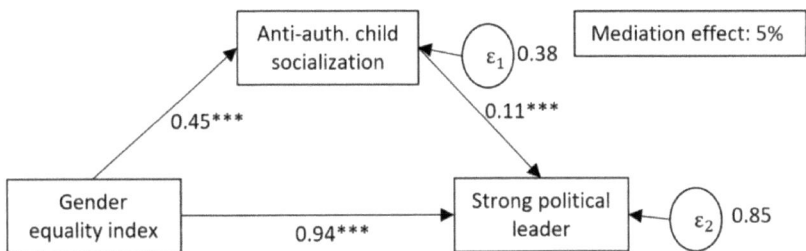

Figure 16 SEM results. Independent variable: gender equality index, mediator: anti-authoritarian attitudes toward childhood socialization. *** = $p < 0.001$

Second, anti-authoritarian values about childhood socialization mediate 5 percent of the relationship between the gender equality index and strong leader perceptions (Figure 16).[15] Thus, people with progressive gender equality values tend to consider tolerance, but not obedience, as important child qualities, which in turn partly explains their more anti-authoritarian attitudes toward political leadership.

Finally, we run the analysis for the domestic violence mediator. We find that the mediation effect equals 9.2 percent (Figure 17).[16] In other words, 9.2 percent of the effect of gender equality values on authoritarian attitudes are mediated by respondents' opposition to domestic violence.

Having run the mediation analyses for the first independent variable, that is, gender equality values, we proceed to run the same analyses using freedom of sexuality values as the independent variable. Figure 18 shows the respective path diagram.

We find that pluralist attitudes mediate 7.1 percent of the relationship between the freedom of sexuality index and strong leader perceptions

---

[15] Robustness check using *medeff* command: 4.9 percent mediation effect.
[16] Result using causal mediation analysis (*medeff* command): 8.7 percent mediation effect.

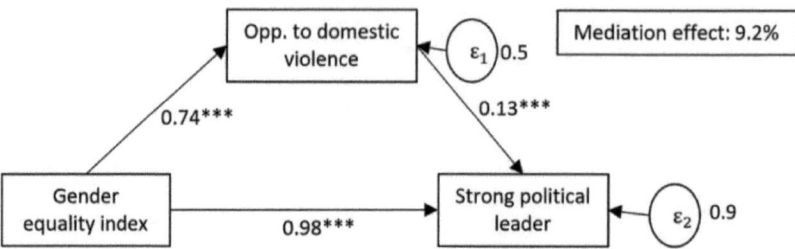

Figure 17 SEM results. Independent variable: gender equality index, mediator: opposition to domestic violence. *** = $p < 0.001$, ** = $p < 0.01$

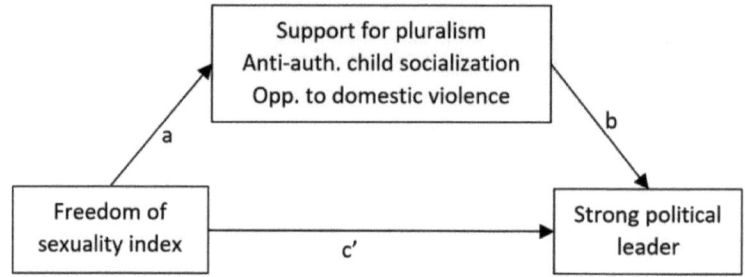

Figure 18 Mediation effects for the relationship between freedom of sexuality values and authoritarianism

Note: *All models control for gender, age, education, importance of God (religiosity), and survey wave (excluded from visualizations for visibility purposes). Survey weights are included; standard errors are clustered by country. The sample comprises WVS waves 3–7 of OECD countries. For the third mediator, that is, opposition to domestic violence, we have data for waves 6–7 only.*

(Figure 19).[17] As regards the mediating effect of democratic values about childhood socialization, we find a slightly stronger effect than we find in our analysis on the gender equality index: 6.3 percent of the relationship between freedom of sexuality values and authoritarian attitudes are mediated by democratic values about childhood socialization (Figure 20).[18] Finally, we find no mediation effects of our third mediator, that is, opposition to domestic violence, for the relationship between the freedom of sexuality index and political authoritarian attitudes (Figure 21).

Overall, our results at the individual level show that, first, gender equality values and freedom of sexuality values are distinct value sets at the individual level. Second, individuals' attitudes toward gender equality and freedom of sexuality are related to individuals' political authoritarianism. These

---

[17] Result using causal mediation analysis (*medeff* command): 6.9 percent mediation effect.
[18] Result using causal mediation analysis (*medeff* command): 6.3 percent mediation effect.

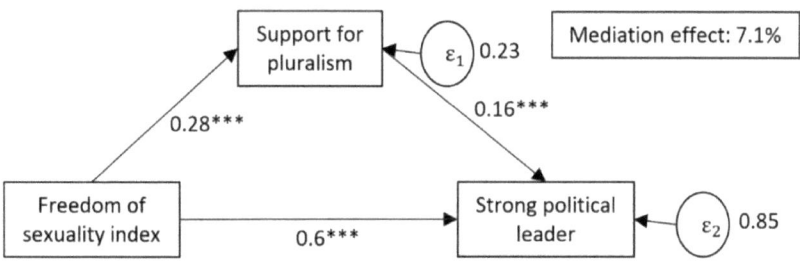

Figure 19 SEM results. Independent variable: freedom of sexuality index, mediator: support for pluralism. *** = $p < 0.001$

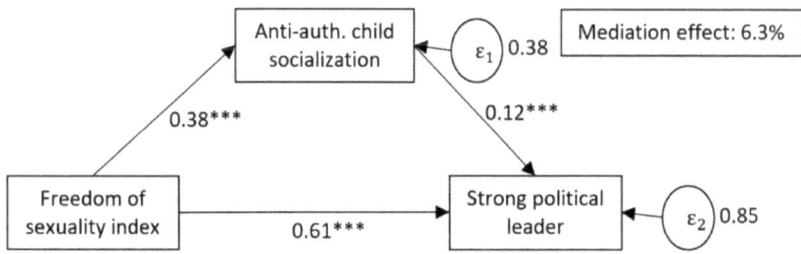

Figure 20 SEM results. Independent variable: freedom of sexuality index, mediator: anti-authoritarian attitudes toward childhood socialization. *** = $p < 0.001$

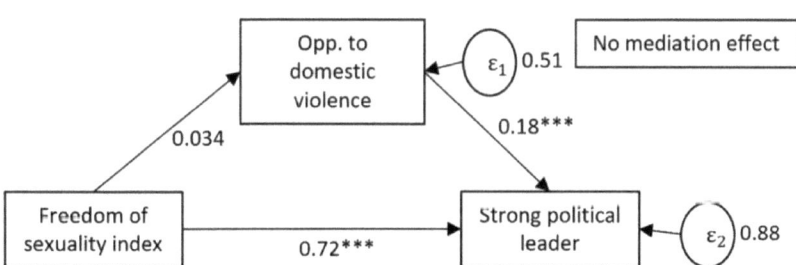

Figure 21 SEM results. Independent variable: freedom of sexuality index, mediator: opposition to domestic violence. *** = $p < 0.001$

relationships are mediated to a small extent by pluralist attitudes and the valuing of democratic childhood socialization for both independent variables. Domestic violence partly mediates the relationship between gender equality attitudes and political authoritarianism, however not the relationship between freedom of sexuality attitudes and political authoritarianism.

Our mediation analyses provide support for our theory that an individuals' gender and sexuality values affect their attitudes toward freedom of speech, democratic socialization in households, violence in the household, and, ultimately, authoritarian political leadership. This is particularly the case for individuals' gender equality values, that is, their beliefs about men's and women's roles in society and the stereotypical nature of men's and women's supposed natures. People who believe that men's careers and education should be prioritized over women's careers and education, and that men should hold positions of power in society, are less likely to consider freedom of speech as important, more likely to consider obedience an important child quality, less likely to consider tolerance an important child quality, and more likely to justify men's violence toward their wives and parents' violence toward their children. It is, however, noteworthy that each of these factors explains only a small part of the relationship between individuals' gender equality values and their political authoritarianism.

In conclusion, our individual-level analysis supports our theory that individuals' gender equality and freedom of sexuality values are significantly related to political authoritarian attitudes. Specifically, individuals' beliefs about men's and women's role in society, gender stereotypes, and individual's sexual self-determination beyond the traditional norm are consequential for their endorsement of political authoritarianism. The more conservative a person's gender and sexuality values, the more likely this person will support an authoritarian political leader. This relationship is stronger for GE values than for FS values. Our findings suggest that a small part of the investigated relationship is explained by the fact that conservative gender equality and freedom of sexuality values are related to lower support for pluralism, more authoritarian attitudes toward childhood socialization, and less opposition to domestic violence. These variables are in turn related to greater support for political authoritarianism. While each of these mechanisms only explains small parts of the relationship between gender equality values, freedom of sexuality values and support for political authoritarianism, they give important insight into how gender and sexuality values likely influence individuals' support or opposition to political authoritarianism.

3 A Theory of How Countries Develop a Culture of GEFS and Political (Anti-)Authoritarianism as Mutually Reinforcing Cultural Processes

This section now turns to the country level and focuses on the bidirectional relationship between GEFS norms and norms related to political authoritarianism. A social norm is here understood as a behavioral rule that applies across various situations, is followed by sufficiently many people in a population, and is enforced through the sanctioning of deviations from it (Bicchieri 2016, pp. 65–66).

We theorize that increasingly progressive GEFS norms among the population increase the population's opposition to political authoritarianism and increasingly conservative GEFS norms in a population increase the population's support for political authoritarian norms for reasons that align with our individual-level expectations. In addition to this direction of influence, we also think that it is plausible that shifts in political authoritarian or anti-authoritarian norms can influence the GEFS norms of a country's population, through institutional changes and signals as well as political elite cues. Thus, at the country level, we expect the relationship between these two sets of norms to be mutually reinforcing.

The section is structured as follows. First, we develop our theory of how progressive or conservative GEFS norms influence political (anti-)authoritarian norms across countries and discuss how this builds on relevant research in political culture. Second, we focus on how shifts in populations' opposition to or support for political authoritarianism can impact their GEFS norms across countries by building on the literatures about institutional signals and political elite cues in norm change. This theoretical section is followed by an empirical section testing the expectations of the relationship between GEFS norms and political authoritarian norms as mutually reinforcing at the country level.

3.1 How GEFS Norms Affect Political (Anti-)Authoritarian Norms

Our individual-level theory developed in Section 2 generates a micro-foundation for understanding how populations develop GEFS norms that influence political authoritarian norms in their countries. In that theory, individuals develop GEFS values based on whether they are embedded in more or less progressive gender structures over their lifecycles. Thus, following this logic but aggregating it to the country level, we argue that populations develop GEFS norms based on the variation in household and community gender and sexuality structures throughout their countries. If patriarchal and heteronormative structures are widespread, the population will face more pressure to conform to hegemonic masculine dominance, which will weaken progressive GEFS norms and strengthen political authoritarian norms. To the contrary, if progressive gender structures are widespread, the population will face more freedom and autonomy in how gender and sexuality structure their identity, expression, and capabilities, which will strengthen progressive GEFS norms and weaken political authoritarian norms.

Under this framework, we contribute to the literature on political culture by theorizing the distinctive role progressive GEFS norms play in strengthening opposition to political authoritarianism across countries. We argue that populations with more progressive GEFS norms are more likely to oppose leadership rooted in and legitimated by the patriarchal structures of hegemonic masculine dominance. Conversely, populations with more conservative GEFS norms will more likely legitimize a form of leadership that conforms with patriarchal structures and hegemonic masculine dominance. Political authoritarianism is rooted in, legitimated by, and sustained by those structures and, thus, progressive GEFS norms will strengthen norms resistant to authoritarian forms of leadership, while conservative GEFS norms will legitimize authoritarian leadership norms. On this front, we contribute to theory with a new mechanism through which GEFS norms potentially strengthen democratic culture by focusing, in particular, on the gendered nature of political authoritarian leadership and, consequently, the importance of gender norms in generating conformity or resistance among populations to that leadership.

While political culture research has indeed considered populations' GEFS norms important to the development of democratic values and the development and quality of democracy across countries (Inglehart and Welzel 2005; Welzel 2013), this research has not theorized or examined how GEFS norms distinctly generate conformity or resistance among populations to political authoritarianism. Instead, the most relevant literature focuses on populations' GEFS norms as fundamental to measuring parts of a larger emancipative value system and considers the role of this broader value system in driving democratic values and achievements across countries (e.g., Welzel 2013). This conceptualization and measurement of populations' emancipative values subsumes attitudes toward GE and FS as attitudes that capture the broader value pillars of equality and freedom of personal choice in a more general system of values.[19]

On the frontier of this research is Welzel's (2013) work on human empowerment and emancipative values. Welzel develops a human empowerment framework to explain variation over time and across the globe in populations' development of widespread and shared human empowering resources that lead to their development of human emancipating values and, in turn, their adoption of human empowering institutions. In this framework, Welzel (2013) conceptualizes emancipative values as an overarching value system that describes populations with high levels of human empowerment. This value system consists of four interrelated and mutually reinforcing dimensions of

---

[19] Subsuming GE and FS attitudes as attitudes that capture the broader value pillars of equality and freedom of personal choice was also the approach in the value system predecessor to emancipative values, known as self-expression values (Inglehart and Welzel 2005).

beliefs that support different aspects of human empowerment labeled voice, equality, choice, and autonomy. Of those, equality is conceptualized as capturing populations' general value and respect for people's right to universal equality of opportunities while choice is conceptualized as capturing populations' general tolerance and respect for people's right to live diverse lifestyles. These concepts are operationalized with data aggregated from individuals' survey responses to the questions on GE and FS in the WVS that we also work with in this Element.

Welzel considers populations' average support of GE fundamental to understanding the general support in countries of the universal equal treatment of people. He considers average support of GE a marker of this given the universal marginalization of women and girls from power and resources in some variety globally, across countries and overtime. Due to the deeply rooted, universal legacy of patriarchy, the progress of valuing human empowerment from an equality perspective can be tracked systematically through the observation of populations' GE norms. Likewise, Welzel considers populations' average support of FS as fundamental to understanding the general support in countries of tolerance and respect for people's right to live diverse lifestyles. He considers average support of FS a marker of this given the universal intolerance and repression of different aspects of FS in some variety globally, across countries and overtime. Similar to the gender equality perspective, due to the deeply rooted, universal legacy of patriarchy, the progress of human empowerment from a choice perspective can be tracked systematically through the observation of populations' FS norms.

This is how the GEFS dimensions of beliefs come to form core pillars of a larger, cultural emancipative value system that varies across countries in this tradition of political culture research. Welzel's theory acknowledges patriarchy as one of the most deeply rooted, universal cultural structures of inequality and repression. He therefore considers measures of GEFS attitudes across countries that show progress from conformity to resistance to patriarchy as particularly indicative of progress in the equality and choice aspects of the cultural emancipative value system.

In addition to the most relevant work on GEFS attitudes, Alexander and Welzel (2017) limit their focus to FS attitudes and argue that opposition to FS is particularly high among supporters of illiberalism in democracies. According to Alexander and Welzel, as a final bastion of conservative practice, defending illiberal sexuality norms is a key defining element of cultural backlash that inspires illiberal challenges to democracy, like right-wing populism. The evidence from Alexander and Welzel's study supports the relationship between illiberal sexuality norms and illiberal regime attitudes across countries.

Building on this political culture literature, we add to the role of GEFS in strengthening countries' emancipative values (Welzel 2013) and progress in liberal values generally (Alexander and Welzel 2017). We contribute to this literature by theorizing and examining the *distinctive role GEFS norms play in strengthening opposition to political authoritarianism across countries*.

3.2 How Political (Anti-)Authoritarian Norms Affect GEFS Norms

So far, we have theorized how progressive or conservative GEFS norms can affect political (anti-)authoritarian norms. In this section, we focus on how political (anti-)authoritarian norms can affect a population's GEFS norms. First, we illustrate how less (more) authoritarian governments have often promoted less (more) conservative GEFS policy in the past. Then, we build on research on social norm change through institutional signals and the literature on political elite cues to theorize mechanisms through which political (anti-)authoritarian norms affect a population's GEFS norms. Finally, we build on research illustrating how mainstream parties can normalize norm-challenging discourse.

3.2.1 How Less Authoritarian Governments Allow for More Progressive GEFS Policymaking, While More Authoritarian Governments Advance More Conservative GEFS Discourse and Policy

Democracy, in combination with women's suffrage, has been argued to foster GEFS (Beer 2009; Anderson 2023). Much of this literature refers to characteristics of democratic institutions that foster GEFS norms, rather than the agency of political elites. Such institutional characteristics include, for instance, a political opportunity structure for women's and LGBTQI+ organizations to organize, and elections allowing these population groups to make their voices heard in the political arena (Beer 2009; Anderson 2023). As women's and LGBTQI+ voices become better represented in politics, this representation may substantively change feminist policy to enhance GE and FS in society. Further, this representation increases women's and LGBTQI+ people's visibility in politics and public discourse. Both of these institutional channels may contribute to more progressive GEFS norms in a society in the long term. Such explanations ascribe a rather passively enabling role in allowing for GEFS norms to develop under democratic leadership. Still, as we develop next, democratic leaders who explicitly emphasize progressive GEFS discourse and policy should also more directly progressively affect GEFS norms, and, generally, democratic leaders are more likely to promote progressive GEFS discourse and policy than authoritarian-leaning leaders.

In contrast, authoritarian-leaning leaders in democratic countries take a more active role in constraining GEFS. There are plenty of examples of authoritarian-leaning leaders, governments, or parties advancing conservative GEFS discourse and policy. Such examples include the US Republicans under Donald Trump, several European radical right parties and their politicians and leaders, as well as authoritarian-leaning leaders such as Recep Erdoğan in Turkey and Jair Bolsonaro in Brazil (Kuhar and Paternotte 2018; Dietze and Roth 2020; Sauer 2020; Spierings 2020; Kaul 2021; Chenoweth and Marks 2022). They tend to use sexist discourse toward women politicians or women in general (Kaul 2021). In terms of policy, they often attack abortion and LGBTQI+ rights, and advance traditional family policy (Akkerman 2015; Dietze and Roth 2020). Why are authoritarian leaders and parties more likely to advance conservative GEFS discourse and policy?

Chenoweth and Marks (2022) argue that "aspiring autocrats and patriarchal authoritarians have good reason to fear women's political participation" (p. 105). The authors claim that women's civil rights not only go hand in hand with democracy but also constitute a precondition for democracy. Thus, women's political involvement goes against authoritarian-leaning leaders' goals. Feminist movements particularly fight "social hierarchies that consolidate power in the hands of the few" and therefore are "a powerful weapon against authoritarianism" (p. 106). The authors thus argue that authoritarian leaders' sexism and misogyny is strategic: "They cannot afford to ignore" feminist movements (p. 106). Ben-Ghiat (2020, p. 8) goes as far as to argue that women and LGBTQI+ people "are as much the strongman's enemies as prosecutors and the press."

Kaul (2021) argues that misogyny is central in legitimizing the aims and forms of governments of contemporary authoritarian-leaning leaders. It is instrumentalized as a political strategy. By constructing women and femininity as inferior, and by ascribing femininity to political opponents, minority groups or specific policy areas like human rights, these leaders legitimize an authoritarian rule. In this discourse, ascribed femininity can for instance refer to ineffectiveness, irrationality, or a lack of autonomy and agency. This strategy is particularly used to silence and devaluate critics.

In reality, contemporary authoritarianism is often closely intertwined with conservatism and nationalism. Misogyny not only helps authoritarians uphold societal hierarchies in general, but also serves to promote the goals of conservatism and nationalism, namely the protection of traditional order and the nation. The aforementioned feminization and consequent devaluation of political opponents, minority groups, or specific policy areas often go hand in hand with a construction of them as threats to the nation and the traditional order (Kaul 2021, p. 1635). In response to these constructed threats, authoritarians can legitimize their dominant "strongmen" behavior and politics (p. 1635): Their strong, masculine leadership serves to enforce societal hierarchies, suppress allegedly feminine threats, and thereby protect the traditional order and nation.

The gender dimensions of nationalism and conservatism further justify misogynist policy. In nationalist ideology, women fulfill the crucial role of ensuring the reproduction of the nation through child-bearing and caretaking, which is used to justify constraining women to the private sphere of the family and household (Yuval-Davis 1997). In conservativism, the traditional order is similarly marked by women's primary responsibility in the family and men's role as provider. Nationalist and conservative discourses complement authoritarian misogyny: Women's alleged primary role as child-bearer and care-taker implies that women are emotional and therefore irrational, soft, and weak, and thus need to be led and dominated by men. Be it with or without the help of nationalist or conservative ideology, authoritarians strategically employ misogyny and traditional "strongmen" masculinity to legitimize their power and politics, and to delegitimize political opponents, minority groups, and policy. While this literature offers a starting point to explaining why authoritarian-leaning leaders currently prioritize gender and sexuality issues, as Bjork-James (2020) argues, more research is needed on "why concerns about gender are animating both white nationalism and authoritarian movements across the globe" (p. 182).

3.2.2 A Political Elite's GEFS Discourse and Policy Influence Its Population's GEFS Norms

The previous section argues that less authoritarian governments allow for more progressive GEFS policymaking. In contrast, authoritarians advance conservative GEFS discourse and policy. What does progressive or conservative GEFS policy-making and political elite discourse do to a population's GEFS norms? To theorize how such discourse and policy affect a population's GEFS norms, we build on the social norms, political elite cues, and radical right normalization literatures.

The social norms literature highlights several institutional mechanisms through which a government's or a political party's discourse and policies can affect social norms. These institutional mechanisms have in common that they influence what is widely considered as an appropriate behavior in a society. Further, the political elite cues literature argues that political parties influence public opinion among their electorates, which may contribute to norm change within specific electorates. Finally, the literature on the normalization of the radical right illustrates how norm change can spread from a norm-challenging party's electorate to more mainstream parties' electorates, ultimately resulting in norm change in society more generally. In the following, we elaborate on these mechanisms explaining how political party and government discourse and policy can affect social norms in a society.

Social Norm Change through Institutional Signals

In political systems marked by regular and fair elections that are generally trusted by the population, governments come into power and political parties' vote share increases or decreases through elections. The social norms literature argues that election results provide information as to how prevalent and legitimate different attitudes are in a society. In other words, election results constitute group summary information to the members of the population, affecting how people perceive the population norm of political party preferences (Tankard and Paluck 2016).

If a party promoting conservative or progressive GEFS discourse and policy increases its vote share or gets into government, voters have reason to assume that an increasing share of the population supports such discourse and policies. This should especially be the case when conservative or progressive GEFS discourse and policy proposals are salient in the party's communication and electoral campaign, as has especially been the case for authoritarian parties as well as New Left or Green parties. For instance, the initial election of US President Donald Trump after an electoral campaign marked by prominent sexist statements signaled to the US population that such sexism is socially accepted insofar as it did not lead (a majority of) his party colleagues to refrain from supporting him or voters to refrain from voting for him. If a population democratically elects an openly sexist president, sexism seems to be endorsed or at least tolerated by a large share of the population. Conversely, the election of women political leaders and parties with many female politicians sends a signal as to the population's general endorsement of women in political leadership. Similarly, the election of parties openly promoting advances in progressive GEFS policy informs the population about the level of public endorsement of progressive GEFS policy.

For parties that enter Parliament for the first time, elections can be particularly important: As these parties enter Parliament, they become represented by a democratically legitimate institution, which legitimizes their political positions (Valentim 2021). The information update provided by elections can serve as an orientation as to how democratically legitimate certain parties are considered in a society. As such, authoritarian parties' electoral breakthroughs can serve to normalize and legitimatize conservative GEFS attitudes in society, and thereby reduce the societal stigma and associated social punishment of expressing such attitudes in contexts where such attitudes break with the previous social norm.

Conversely, the electoral breakthroughs of New Left and Green parties in Western European democracies, with progressive GEFS agendas, may exemplify instances of electoral breakthroughs of norm-challenging parties with progressive GEFS stances. The fact that norm-challenging attitudes are newly represented in a widely trusted, democratically legitimate political institution can signal that these attitudes are generally more accepted in society.

An important feature of election results is that they constitute widely available information. Therefore, the information update should generally reach a whole population rather than just subgroups of it, which is a crucial part of social norm change (Bicchieri 2016, p. 110; Tankard and Paluck 2016). Individuals can trust that other members of society have received the same information and updated their perceptions of the social norm accordingly. The social risk of being a "first mover," that is, the first person to act upon the new social norm, is reduced when a population collectively is informed and potentially changes its expectations about the social norm (Bicchieri 2016, pp. 109–110). As Bicchieri (2016, p. 119) argues, "to feel safe in adopting new behaviors, individuals must come to believe that no negative sanctions will follow, which means that so many others have abandoned the old ways, that punishing them all would be ineffective or irrelevant."

By updating the commonly accepted information about political preferences in society, election results can strengthen such feelings of safety: If a large enough population group supports a party with norm-challenging GEFS positions, the social sanctioning of individuals who support the party and hold norm-challenging GEFS attitudes will become ineffective or irrelevant at the societal level. The widespread nature of information on election results ensures that most people roughly know about the support levels for successful norm-challenging parties in a society. If it is safe to assume that most people know about it, people with norm-challenging GEFS attitudes should feel safer to express these attitudes without being sanctioned for it, which in turn should lead to a more widespread normalization of these attitudes among these groups.

Beyond elections, electoral breakthroughs and rising vote shares, Tankard and Paluck (2016) and Bicchieri (2016, p. 143) highlight the role of other institutions in social norm change. While elections only happen every few years, other institutions can more consistently exert influence on collective perceptions of social norms. Education and the mass media, as well as new government legislation, judicial rulings, or economic interventions can contribute to norm change if these institutions are generally trusted and considered legitimate. Institutional signals influence collective expectations of what is considered an appropriate behavior. Changes in legislation and economic incentives set a framework for appropriate behavior. The mass media and schooling further influence common perceptions of appropriate behavior and common knowledge of these perceptions. Especially for the case of mass media coverage, individual people can be sure that many others have received the information conveyed by the mass media on what is considered appropriate behavior, reducing the risk of being socially punished for acting accordingly (Arias 2019).

All these institutions constitute channels through which governments can influence their populations' GEFS norms, especially if the governments are trusted. For instance, legislation on same-sex marriage or adoption can affect people's perceptions of the appropriateness of same-sex marriage or adoption. Similarly, changes in economic incentives, for instance in family taxation, can affect people's perceptions of the appropriate division of labor in a family. The government can further influence schooling: For instance, governments may decide to include liberal sex education in the curriculum, or not. Such decisions can affect the expectations of what is appropriate behavior of a whole generation of school children.

Finally, especially in more authoritarian contexts where freedom of press is more constrained, governments can influence mass media coverage. The Hungarian government's ban on LGBQTI+ content in media targeting children and youth constitutes an example of such influence. But even in contexts where norm-challenging parties cannot directly influence media coverage, the mass media will likely report and comment on the norm-breaking discourse or policymaking and thereby provide information as to how wide-spread and socially accepted such behavior is. The social norm literature thus highlights several institutional mechanisms that can explain how a government's or a political party's discourse or policy can lead to social norm change.

Political Parties' Influence on Voters' Opinion

In addition, the public opinion literature argues that there is a link between political elites' positions and public opinion, as voters tend to adopt the positions of their preferred parties (Zaller 1992; Leeper and Slothuus 2014). Beyond the previously discussed mechanism of media coverage on political discourse and policymaking, this literature highlights mechanisms such as framing and motivated reasoning to explain the link between political elites and public opinion.

The framing mechanism implies that, depending on how a party frames a political issue, it influences how its voters understand the relevance and content of the issue (Slothuus and De Vreese 2010). For instance, parties may choose to emphasize GEFS issues, which can in turn influence how much importance voters ascribe to these issues. Parties can further decide to differently portray

GEFS issues' relevance. For instance, feminist-leaning parties may frame GEFS issues as a matter of social justice between men and women or cis-hetero and LGBTQI+ people. In contrast, conservative actors have portrayed progressive GEFS policy issues as a colonial policy agenda imposed by Western organizations (Korolczuk and Graff 2018; Rawłuszko 2019), and a threat to freedom of expression or even human civilization as a whole (Kuhar and Paternotte 2018). Whether and how political elites discuss GEFS issues is likely to affect how voters perceive those issues. In support of this argument, Off (2023) shows that German radical right voters frame GEFS issues in similar ways as the party they support.

Another mechanism explaining why people adapt their preferred parties' positions is motivated reasoning. Motivated reasoning describes individuals' own efforts to hold attitudes and argue for these attitudes in line with their preferred parties' positions (Petersen et al. 2013; Leeper and Slothuus 2014). As political parties put forward their positions, their voters will make an effort to find arguments that support these positions in order to defend and thereby confirm, rather than to refute, their previous commitment to the party. For instance, a left-leaning party that may have traditionally focused largely on socioeconomic equality may change to emphasize and promote not only socioeconomic gender equality but also engage with issues like gender-based violence or LGBTQI+ rights. In contrast, an authoritarian-leaning party may have previously focused on the immigration issue, and then expanded its agenda to emphasize conservative family values and anti-LGBTQI+ positions as well. The motivated reasoning hypothesis predicts that the partisans of these respective parties will likely update their own attitudes according to their parties' new positions, especially if these new positions are relatively in line with their previous positions.

In contrast to the social norm literature focusing on norm changes in society as a whole, the literature on political elite influence particularly explains partisans' attitude formation, and, consequently, potential norm changes only within a party's electorate. For instance, the sexist discourse of US President Donald Trump (Kaul 2021) may have led to a spread and normalization of sexism among people who identified as Republicans already before Trump's first presidential candidacy. In fact, research shows that conservative GEFS attitudes predicted Trump voting in Trump's first presidential candidacy more so than it predicted Republican voting in previous elections (Cassese and Barnes 2019). This finding suggests that conservative GEFS values were more normalized and/or more salient among Republicans in the 2016 Trump election than in previous elections. Similarly, Green parties' progressive GEFS discourse and policy proposals may have resulted in the spread of such values among voters of Green parties in particular – even if they initially voted for the parties for environmentalist concerns.

In contrast, Trump's sexism will unlikely have contributed to a spread or normalization of sexist attitudes among Democratic voters. Rather, the opposite may have occurred: Democrats' counter-reactions to Trump's sexism may have resulted in elite polarization between Republicans and Democrats. Elite polarization has in turn been shown to stimulate partisan motivated reasoning (Druckman, Peterson and Slothuus 2013), which should then lead to increased mass polarization between Democratic and Republican voters. As Republicans may have adapted increasingly conservative GEFS norms, Democrats' GEFS norms may have remained unchanged or become increasingly progressive. This example illustrates that political parties and politicians may induce norm change among their partisans, however not among political opponents' voters.

Other parties' voters' reactions to norm change within a partisan group can depend on how other parties react to the norm-challenging party. In contrast to the aforementioned example of the United States in which the established Republican Party challenged societal norms, many European democracies are marked by weaker partisanship and proportional representation systems, which can facilitate the rise of new norm-challenging parties such as New Left/ Green parties or radical right parties. Considering radical right parties as relatively new, norm-challenging parties, the literature on the normalization of radical right parties helps explain how the rise of a norm-challenging party can change the political mainstream and thereby potentially affect norms in society more generally.

Mainstream Parties' Normalization of Norm-challenging Parties

Abou-Chadi and Krause (2018) find that the success of radical right parties has changed the political positions of both mainstream left-wing and mainstream right-wing parties. In the case of radical right parties, the position changes regard positions on immigration and multiculturalism. Because radical right parties often "own" anti-immigration and nationalist stances, these are the issues that are perceived as the drivers of voters' transitions to the radical right. As many examples in European countries have shown, to win back their former voters, mainstream parties change their positions on these issues to become more similar to the radical right. In a similar logic, mainstream parties would change their stances to become more environmentalist in response to the rise of Green parties. Because Green parties "own" the issue of environmentalism, and because some voters shifted from mainstream parties to Green parties, mainstream parties should adapt their stances toward more environment-friendly ones.

Thus, while norm-challenging parties may directly affect expectations of what is a socially acceptable or desirable attitude only among their own electorates, the normalization of norm-challenging parties' positions among mainstream parties may affect parts of the mainstream electorate, too. Down and Han (2020) argue that mainstream parties' adaptation of radical right positions on immigration legitimizes these positions and thereby increases radical right support in a population. The case of norm-challenging radical right parties' anti-immigration stances and mainstream parties' adaptation of these positions illustrates how norm-challengers can become normalized among political elites, and consequently, in society more generally.

While research illustrates this process of normalizing political stances that constitute norm-challenging parties' most important issues, such as immigration or the environment in the case of radical right or Green parties, less is known about whether this holds for less salient positions of norm-challenging parties, such as GEFS positions. As norm-challenging parties expand their political agenda to include GEFS issues, they politicize these issues and promote mostly stances related to gender and sexuality identity (Abou-Chadi, Breyer, and Gessler 2021). For the case of rising radical right parties with conservative GEFS stances, Weeks and Allen (2022) show that European mainstream parties accommodate this not by entirely adapting the radical right's conservative GEFS stances but by shifting their attention away from GEFS issues and toward socioeconomic issues. If mainstream parties do address GEFS issues, the authors show that they increasingly accommodate the radical right's discourse framing immigration as a threat to gender equality. The analysis suggests that, when norm-challenging parties rise, mainstream parties may partly accommodate their stances on GEFS issues, potentially contributing to a normalization of their more conservative GEFS stances.

Overall, the previously discussed literatures suggest four mechanisms to explain how the rise of more norm-challenging elites and the sway they have over government and discourse can influence a society's GEFS norms. First, the literature on social norm change highlights the role of *institutional signals* such as election results, parliamentary representation, media coverage, or education in changing norms. Second, research on political elites' influence on public opinion suggests that *motivated reasoning* makes voters adjust to the positions of their preferred political parties. Therefore, the rise of a norm-challenging party with particular GEFS stances can contribute to normalizing such stances among the party's electorate. Third, this literature argues that political parties' *framing* of political issues influences how voters perceive the issue. Finally, the literature on *radical right normalization* suggests that mainstream parties partly accommodate stances of norm-challenging parties, including on GEFS issues, thereby contributing to a normalization of such stances among mainstream electorates, too.

3.3 In a Nutshell: Our Theory of a Mutually Reinforcing Relationship between Countries' GEFS Norms and Political Authoritarian Norms

This section developed the Element's theory of how countries develop a culture of GEFS and opposition to political authoritarianism as mutually reinforcing cultural processes. In our focus on the influence of populations' GEFS norms on political (anti-)authoritarian norms, we theorize that increasingly progressive (or conservative) GEFS norms among the population increase the population's opposition to (or support of) political authoritarianism for reasons that align with our individual-level theory. On this front, we contribute theoretically by developing a new mechanism through which GEFS norms strengthen democratic culture by focusing on the gendered nature of political authoritarian leadership and, consequently, the importance of gender norms in generating conformity or resistance among populations to that leadership. We argue that populations with higher levels of GEFS norms are more likely to oppose leadership rooted in and legitimated by the patriarchal structures of hegemonic masculine dominance. Political authoritarianism is rooted in, legitimated by, and sustained by those structures and, thus, progress in GEFS norms will strengthen norms resistant to that form of political leadership.

In our focus on the influence of populations' (anti-)authoritarian norms on GEFS norms, we argue that one way this works is through improving support of democratic institutionalization if populations become less authoritarian or weakening support of democratic institutionalization if populations become more authoritarian. In addition to this, we chart new theoretical ground by theorizing how the shift in authoritarian norms potentially negatively influences GEFS norms through explicit mobilization for or against GE and FS by the norm-challenging political actors empowered by (anti-)authoritarian shifts in democracies. Here, we argue that the rise of norm-challenging political elites promoting conservative or progressive GEFS stances can contribute to the normalization of such GEFS stances in the population. Building on the literatures about social norm change through institutional signals, political elites, and cue-taking, as well as the normalization of the radical right, we outline mechanisms explaining how political elites with progressive or conservative GEFS stances can affect GEFS norms in the population. Combining our theoretical arguments about the two directions of influence between GEFS norms and political (anti-)authoritarian norms, we outline a theoretical framework for expecting a mutually reinforcing relationship between a country's population's GEFS norms and its political (anti-)authoritarian norms. In the following section, we provide first evidence in support of this mutually reinforcing relationship.

4 An Analysis of GEFS Norms and Political (Anti-)Authoritarian Norms as Mutually Reinforcing

To analyze the relationship between GEFS norms and political (anti-)authoritarian norms at the aggregate country level, we take information from all respondents living in the same country and take the mean values of their attitudes. While we lose a lot of information on the variation of attitudes within a country, we hope to gain information about countries' norms. How progressive or conservative is a country, on average, in terms of its GEFS norms? To what extent is political authoritarianism, on average, supported or rejected? While various country-level indicators, such as a country's gender pay gap, gender parity in power positions, laws about abortion, divorce or homosexuality, or political institutions can give important insights into these questions, we are interested in the more informal, social dimensions of what is considered the norm and socially accepted in society. By moving from the individual to the aggregate level, we thus intend to capture the relationship between GEFS norms in a society and a society's political (anti-)authoritarian norms more generally. Aggregating the information to the country level further allows us to compare across different countries and over the time period of the different survey waves from 1995 to 2022. With information on variation in the level of countries' GEFS norms and political (anti-)authoritarian norms over an earlier and later time point, we can empirically examine to what extent these norms are mutually reinforcing over time, which we are not able to do with the individual-level data, because we do not have data on the same individuals over time. In this case, we are able to gain this unique insight into the relationship between the two sets of norms on the country level.

We expect a mutually reinforcing relationship between a country's GEFS norms and its political (anti-)authoritarian norms: On the one hand, a country's GEFS norms should affect political (anti-)authoritarian norms. On the other hand, political (anti-)authoritarian norms should affect its GEFS norms. In the previous theory section, we outlined the mechanisms through which we expect this circular relationship to take effect. In the following, we provide first evidence that supports the expectation of a mutually reinforcing relationship between these two sets of norms.

4.1 The Strategy for Testing the Expectation of a Mutually Reinforcing Relationship

As we do in the individual-level analysis, we use data from the World Value Survey from 28 OECD countries and waves 3–7 (Inglehart et al. 2020). We aggregate the data from the individual to the mean country level to capture what we describe as norms of GEFS and political (anti-)authoritarianism. As control variables, we use country-level data on GDP per capita from the Quality of Government dataset (Teorell et al. 2023) to capture economic development. We further aggregate the previously used individual-level WVS measure for religiosity, namely the importance ascribed to God, to capture a country's religious norms. Finally, we use the V-Dem Electoral Democracy Index (Coppedge et al. 2021) corresponding to each WVS survey wave's first year of data collection (1995 for wave 3, 1999 for wave 4, etc.) to control for a country's level of democracy. Using these control variables, we intend to capture the most important influences on an OECD country's GEFS and political (anti-)authoritarian norms, including time trends, and economic, political and cultural institutions affecting the development of those norms.[20]

Following our work at the individual-level, we look at countries' GE indexes and FS indexes separately. The GE and FS indexes that we use for our country-level analysis range from 0 to 1, where higher values equal a more progressive culture of GE and FS. The indexes are composed of the same 6 indicators that we previously used to compile the GE and FS indexes at the individual level: Agreement with the statements that (1) men's jobs should be prioritized when jobs are scarce, (2) men's university education is more important than women's, (3) men make better political leaders; as well as assessments about how justifiable it is to (4) be homosexual, (5) have an abortion, and (6) have a divorce. For each country and time period, we compute the means of all respondents' answers to these indicators and add up these mean values to construct the country-level GE and FS indexes (Cronbach's alpha GE: 0.9202; Cronbach's alpha FS: 0.9225). Figures 22 and 23 show the pooled distributions of the GE and FS indexes at the country level.

Figures 22 and 23 show a pattern similar to the individual level at the country level: populations are on average more supportive of GE compared to FS and countries vary more in their support of FS compared to GE. Thus, across our sample of countries and time points, we observe more variation in support for FS compared to GE. Unlike at the individual level, our number of observations is much more limited at the country level. This likely limits the potential impact

---

[20] See Online Appendix III for summary statistics for the country-level variables and pairwise correlations between variables measured at the country level.

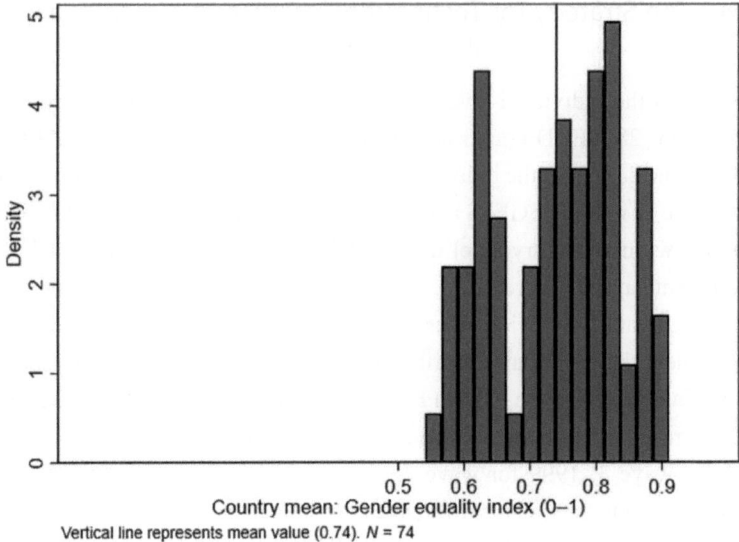

Figure 22 Pooled distribution of the GE index at the country level

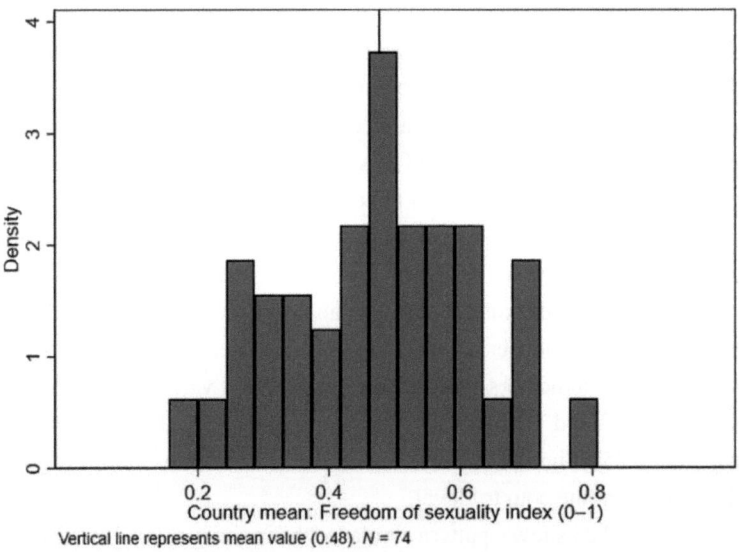

Figure 23 Pooled distribution of the FS index at the country level

of the GE index compared to the FS index on political (anti-)authoritarian attitudes at the country level. This is a drawback of working with country averages to measure the influence of the GE and FS norms on political (anti-)authoritarian norms across economically advanced democracies. We would pick up more variation in these norms, particularly in GE norms, with more nuanced regional data that captured the variation in these norms within countries. This more nuanced variation would align better with our theoretical expectations that the gender structures that individuals are embedded in vary profoundly at the more local, community level. Conversely, the national-level analysis better reflects our argument that political elites can influence norms because national-level politics tends to be more visible than regional-level politics. While an analysis of both the regional and the national levels would thus be ideal, we limit ourselves to a national-level analysis given data availability.

Our second variable of interest is the aggregate level of political (anti-)authoritarianism by country and time period. Again, we rely on the same survey indicator as we do in our individual-level analysis: Respondents' assessment of a political system that has "a strong leader who does not have to bother with parliament and elections" as very good, fairly good, bad, or very bad. To compute our country-level measure of political (anti-)authoritarianism, for each country and time period, we take the mean of all respondents' response values. To ensure comparability of our two main variables' coefficients, we further rescale the political authoritarianism variable as to range from 0 to 1, where 0 equals most authoritarian norms and 1 equals least authoritarian norms. Figure 24 shows the distributions of our country-level measure of political authoritarianism.

Part of our theoretical expectations include a positive relationship between the GE and FS indexes and our measure of political anti-authoritarianism, where

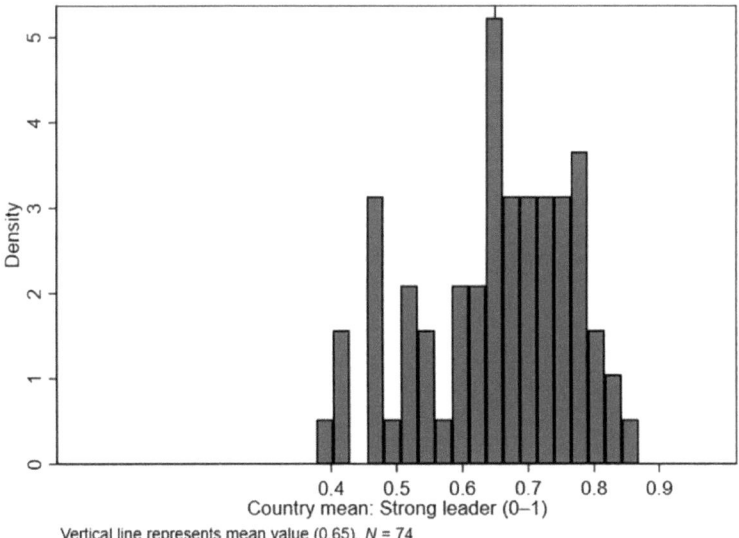

Figure 24 Pooled distribution of political anti-authoritarianism at the country level

more progressive GE and FS norms are related to less authoritarian norms in a society. Figures 25 and 26 show scatterplots and the results of a locally weighted regression (lowess) smoothing of the GE and FS indexes and strong leader perceptions at the country level, supporting our expectation about a positive relationship between the variables and anti-authoritarian leader perceptions. Note, however, that these scatterplots do not allow for conclusions about the direction of effect at play between these variables. While the plots visualize their relationships in a descriptive way, all previously theorized directions of effect may be at play: Conservative (progressive) GEFS norms affecting political (anti-)authoritarian norms, and vice versa. The following inferential analysis will allude more to the direction of effects at play in this relationship of variables.

To test our theoretical argument about the mutually reinforcing relationship between GEFS norms and political (anti-)authoritarian norms, we apply seemingly unrelated regression (SUR) analyses with lagged variables. SUR analysis allows the simultaneous estimation of two regression models while allowing for their error terms to be correlated. In applying this method, we take inspiration from previous work testing similar arguments on relationships that take the form of virtuous/ vicious cycles between two variables (e.g., Alexander 2012; Bystrov 2014).

SUR analyses test the relationship between two variables at two different time points. Essentially, variable 1 at time t is regressed on variable 2 at $t-1$.

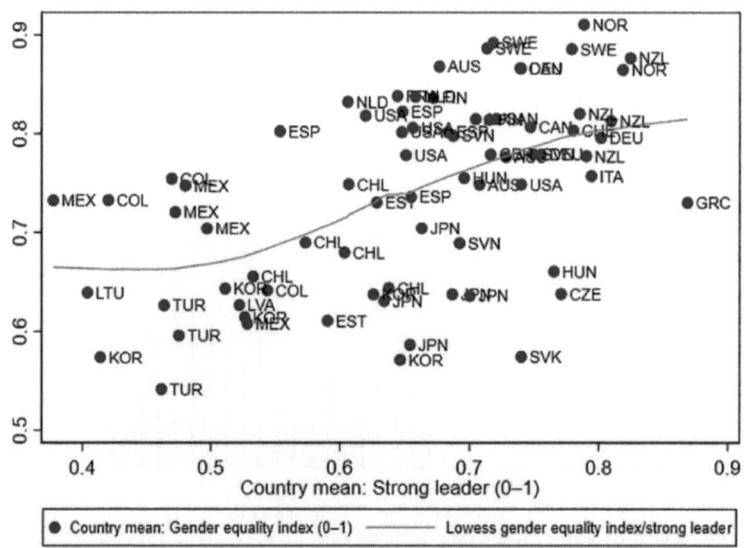

Figure 25 Scatterplot and lowess smoothing of the GE index and political (anti-)authoritarianism at the country level

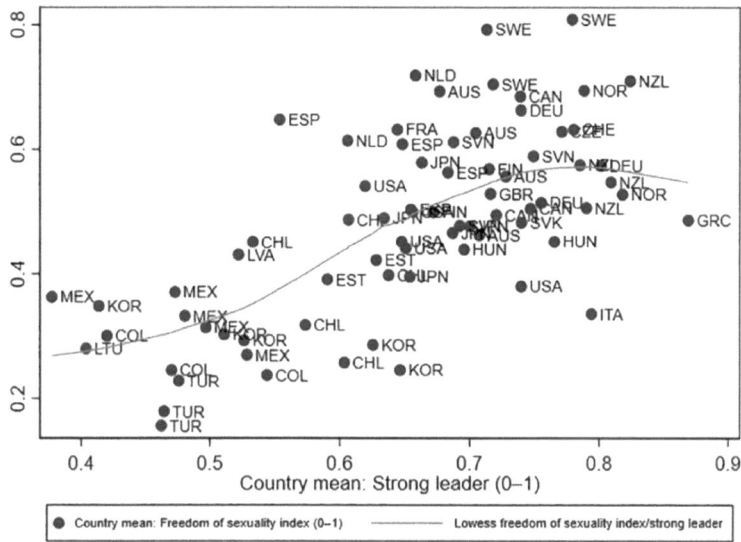

Figure 26 Scatterplot and lowess smoothing of the FS index and political (anti-)authoritarianism at the country level

Simultaneously, variable 2 at time t is regressed on variable 1 at $t-1$. Thus, we are able to test whether a country's GE and FS norms at an observed point in time (e.g., survey wave 3) are related to its political (anti-)authoritarian norms at the subsequent observed point in time (e.g., survey wave 4). At the same time, in line with our argument about a mutually reinforcing relationship, we test whether the country's political (anti-)authoritarian norms at the first observed point in time are related to its GE and FS norms at the second observed point in time. Allowing the error terms to be correlated takes into account that the two processes tested in the two regression models are theorized as mutually reinforcing, and thus, related to each other.

Due to the need for a time lag, country-wave observations without observations at preceding survey waves are dropped from our sample used for the SUR analysis. Because we rely on lagged variables to specify the mutually reinforcing relationship between the GE and FS indexes and our measure of political authoritarianism, we can only include countries with at least two subsequent observations across survey waves. This reduces the number of countries included in the analysis from 28 ($N = 74$) to 15 ($N = 36$), depending on the model specification.

The small sample size of $N = 74$ or $N = 36$ analyzed at the country level carries at least three risks. First, in small samples, extreme cases exert a greater influence on the results. While in large samples, outliers do not affect the results as much, this can be the case in smaller samples, where each observation is more influential. However, visual inspection of the above and below scatterplots does not point to any striking outlier. We therefore do not worry about influential outliers in this analysis. Second, we risk overfitting our models, resulting in imprecise estimates. To avoid overfitting our models, we include the control variables separately in several models rather than altogether in one model. Finally, small sample sizes imply that we should not extrapolate our findings to a greater population. Our results may be specific to the analyzed sample only and not apply to other countries. However, given the variety of countries covered in the analysis, and the large number of people residing in these countries, we believe that our results are relevant even if only applicable to the analyzed countries.

Figures 27 and 28 show scatterplots and lowess smoothings of the country-level GE and FS indexes and political (anti-)authoritarianism of the reduced sample used for the SUR analysis ($N = 36$). The scatterplots further indicate which country-wave observations are included in the sample. Despite the small sample size, the sample includes OECD countries from different world regions, such as Sweden, Germany, and Spain in Europe, New Zealand in Oceania, South Korea and Japan in East Asia, Turkey in the Middle East, the USA in North America, and Mexico and Colombia in Latin America, among others. The scatterplots support our argument about a positive relationship between

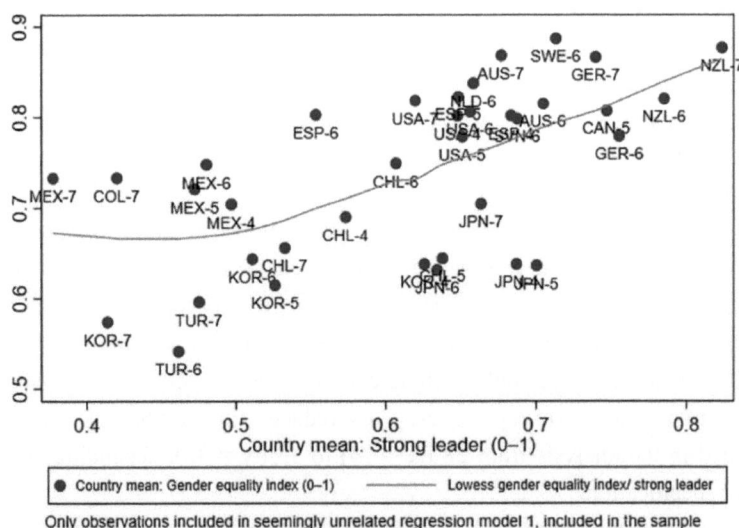

Figure 27 Scatterplot and lowess smoothing of the GE index and political (anti-)authoritarianism at the country level, reduced sample

Attitudes toward Political Authoritarianism 61

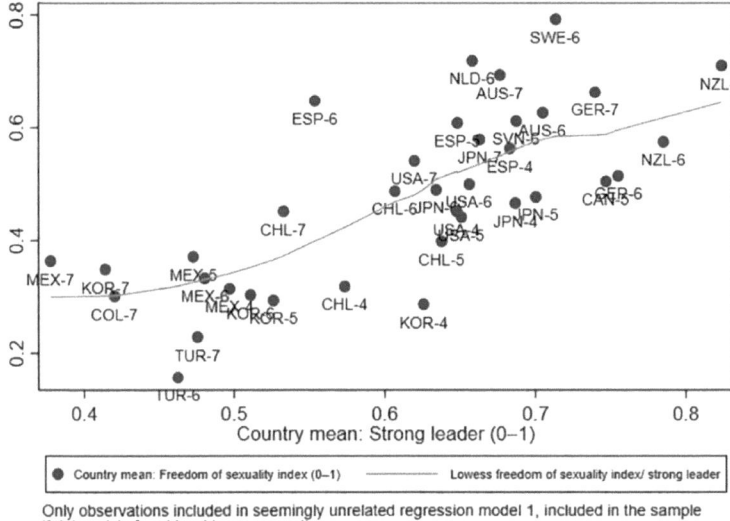

Figure 28 Scatterplot and lowess smoothing of the FS index and political (anti-)authoritarianism at the country level, reduced sample

GEFS norms and the culture of political (anti-)authoritarianism. However, as we noted earlier, they do not allow for any conclusions on the direction of effects in the described relationships.

Note, that while the small sample implies a lack of statistical power, the fact that we still find significant effects in our following analysis further strengthens the support for our hypothesis. To partly address the lack of statistical power, we proceed by including our control variables separately in the following statistical model, rather than adding them to the model successively.

Tables 1 and 2 show the results of the SUR analysis with time lags, wherein the GE and FS indexes and strong political leader perceptions are both used as dependent variables, and the respective other variable's time lag is used as the main independent variable. Thus, in the upper part of the tables, strong political leader perceptions at t are regressed on the GE and FS indexes at $t-1$. Simultaneously, in the lower part of the tables, the GE and FS indexes at t are regressed on strong political leader perceptions at $t-1$. As mentioned earlier, we include relevant control variables separately to avoid problems with statistical power.

Given the coding of the GE and FS indexes as running from a conservative country average (closer to 0) to a progressive country average (closer to 1), and the measure of strong leader perceptions as running from a supportive country average (closer to 0) to an opposing country average (closer to 1), the coefficients depict,

Table 1 Results of SUR analyses of the GE index and strong leader perceptions, with time lags

	(1)	(2)	(3)	(4)
DV: Country mean: Against strong leadership (0–1)				
Country mean: GE index ($t-1$, 0–1)	0.860***	0.640**	0.442	0.385
	(0.19)	(0.20)	(0.25)	(0.28)
Country mean: Importance of God		−0.283**		
		(0.09)		
Real GDP per capita in 2011 USD			0.000*	
			(0.00)	
V-Dem electoral democracy index				0.402
				(0.22)
Constant	−0.053	0.273	0.107	−0.013
	(0.15)	(0.17)	(0.15)	(0.19)
R2	0.252	0.542	0.481	0.447
DV: Country mean: GE index (0–1)				
Country mean: Against strong leadership ($t-1$, 0–1)	0.726***	0.896***	0.597***	0.622**
	(0.13)	(0.15)	(0.16)	(0.20)
Country mean: Importance of God		0.178		
		(0.11)		
Real GDP per capita in 2011 USD			0.000	
			(0.00)	
V-Dem electoral democracy index				0.002
				(0.17)
Constant	0.302**	0.095	0.362**	0.364**
	(0.09)	(0.14)	(0.11)	(0.13)
R2	0.398	0.455	0.427	0.421
N (obs.)	36	36	36	36
N (countries)	15	15	15	15

*Standard errors in parentheses; * $p < 0.05$ ** $p < 0.01$, *** $p < 0.001$; seemingly unrelated regression models, standard errors clustered at the country-level, controlling for survey wave; sample: 15 OECD countries, WVS waves 3–7.*

first, how countries' more progressive average GE and FS norms at an earlier time point are related to countries' higher average opposition to a strong leader at a later time point. Second, the coefficients depict how countries' stronger average

Table 2 Results of SUR analyses of the FS index and strong leader perceptions, with time lags

	(1)	(2)	(3)	(4)
DV: Country mean: Against strong leadership (0–1)				
Country mean: FS index ($t-1$, 0–1)	0.701***	0.606***	0.569***	0.614***
	(0.12)	(0.13)	(0.13)	(0.12)
Country mean: Importance of God		−0.061		
		(0.09)		
Real GDP per capita in 2011 USD			0.000	
			(0.00)	
V-Dem electoral democracy index				0.078
				(0.19)
Constant	0.278***	0.353***	0.272***	0.255
	(0.06)	(0.09)	(0.06)	(0.13)
R2	0.561	0.588	0.615	0.584
DV: Country mean: FS index (0–1)				
Country mean: Against strong leadership ($t-1$, 0–1)	1.288***	1.054***	1.164***	1.044***
	(0.14)	(0.26)	(0.20)	(0.20)
Country mean: Importance of God		−0.145		
		(0.15)		
Real GDP per capita in 2011 USD			0.000	
			(0.00)	
V-Dem electoral democracy index				0.217
				(0.15)
Constant	−0.293**	−0.067	−0.254*	−0.311**
	(0.09)	(0.24)	(0.10)	(0.10)
R2	0.642	0.683	0.657	0.677
N (obs.)	36	36	36	36
N (countries)	15	15	15	15

*Standard errors in parentheses; * $p < 0.05$ ** $p < 0.01$, *** $p < 0.001$; seemingly unrelated regression models, standard errors clustered at the country-level, controlling for survey wave; sample: 15 OECD countries, WVS waves 3–7.*

opposition to a strong leader at an earlier time point is related to countries' more progressive average GE and FS norms at a later time point. Note that the direction of effects is an artifact of our coding of the variables. If we were to reverse-code our variables, these coefficients would thus show how more conservative GE and FS norms are related to higher support for strong political leadership at a later time point, and how higher support for strong political leadership is related to more conservative GE and FS norms at a later time point.

The results presented in Tables 1 and 2 support our theoretical argument that GEFS norms and political (anti-)authoritarian norms at the country level are strongly related to each other and mutually reinforcing. Recall that, at the individual level, we found that GE values are more strongly and consistently related to political authoritarianism. In contrast, Tables 1 and 2 show that, at the country level, FS norms are more strongly and more consistently related to political authoritarianism. Depending on the different model specifications, a full-range increase from 0 to 1 in the FS index at $t-1$ is related to an increase in political anti-authoritarian attitudes at t by between 0.569 units (p-value < 0.001, model 3 in Table 2) and 0.701 units (p-value < 0.001, model 1 in Table 2). In comparison, the effect of the GE index at $t-1$ on political anti-authoritarianism at t is not robust to the inclusion of GDP or the electoral democracy index in the model (see Table 1).[21]

In other words, in a hypothetical scenario in which a country's FS norms in one survey wave move from the theoretical minimum value of 0 to the theoretical maximum value of 1 on the FS index, we would expect the society in that country to become significantly less authoritarian in the subsequent survey wave observed around 4–5 years later. Our most conservative estimate (model 3, Table 2) suggests that this country's society would become 0.569 units less authoritarian, where one unit equals the full range from 0 (most authoritarian) to 1 (least authoritarian).

In fact, a 0.569-unit increase in political anti-authoritarian norms constitutes a larger effect than moving from the most authoritarian society in our sample (Mexico in survey wave 7, scoring 0.377) to the least authoritarian society in our sample (Greece in survey wave 7, scoring 0.868). In reality, no observations in our sample score 0 or 1 on the FS index: the actual minimum and maximum values in our sample are 0.156 for Turkey in survey wave 6,[22] and 0.809 for Sweden in survey wave 5, respectively. A one-unit increase in the FS index is

---

[21] As we note earlier, we expected this given that among our sample of countries, populations were generally on average more supportive of GE over the two time points and there was less variation in the GE index compared to the FS index.

[22] To test whether our results are driven by the observations from Turkey, we reran our analyses excluding all observations from Turkey. The effects change only little in magnitude and not in significance or direction of effects, demonstrating that our conclusions hold when excluding Turkey from the analysis (see Online Appendix IV).

therefore just a hypothetical scenario. Still, the effect size of 0.569 units is equal to almost 5 standard deviations in political authoritarianism at the country level and thus highly significant in magnitude.

Simultaneously, the lower parts of Tables 1 and 2 show how political (anti-)authoritarian norms at time $t-1$ are related to a country's GEFS norms at time t. For GE norms (Table 1), the results show that a hypothetical full-range increase from 0 to 1 in political anti-authoritarian norms at $t-1$ is related to an increase in the GE index at t by between 0.597 units (p-value < 0.001, model 3 in Table 1) and 0.896 units (p-value < 0.001, model 2 in Table 1). In contrast to the inverse direction of effect, the effects of political anti-authoritarian norms on GE norms are robust to all model specifications. Again, it is noteworthy that a one-unit increase in political (anti-)authoritarianism is a hypothetical scenario. Still, the effect size is considerable, with our most conservative estimate of 0.597 units equaling more than 6 standard deviations in the GE index.

Again, the effects are stronger for FS norms. Table 2 shows that a hypothetical full-range increase from 0 to 1 in political anti-authoritarian norms at $t-1$ is related to an increase in the FS index at t by between 1.044 units (p-value < 0.001, model 4 in Table 2) and 1.288 units (p-value < 0.001, model 1 in Table 2). The more conservative coefficient of 1.044 equals almost 7 standard deviations in the FS index.

Effectively, these results suggest that a country's political (anti-)authoritarian norms at an observed point in time will affect the country's GEFS norms around four or five years later, where less authoritarian norms will lead to more progressive GEFS norms and more authoritarian norms will lead to more conservative GEFS norms. While our findings point to generally large effect sizes, the relationship appears to be stronger for FS norms than for GE norms at the country level. In other words, our results suggest that, as a society turns less (more) politically authoritarian, especially freedom of sexuality but also gender equality will be positively (negatively) affected.

Finally, as a robustness check for our SUR analyses, we run panel regressions of all 28 OECD countries in the sample across waves 3–7 (unbalanced panel, $n = 74$) without time lags. While panel regression analysis allows us to test how the variables are related to each other, it does not allow us to test the hypothesis about a mutually reinforcing relationship in a meaningful way, as it does not allow for error terms to be correlated and we do not include time-lagged variables. However, panel regression analysis allows us to take advantage of the greater statistical power provided in our sample. Given their respective advantages and disadvantages, we believe that conducting both SUR with time lags and panel regression analysis without time lags constitute our best possible ways to derive robust conclusions on the relationship between a country's GEFS norms and political (anti-)authoritarian norms.

Tables 3 and 4 show panel regression analyses further supporting the argument that FS norms and political (anti-)authoritarian norms are related to each other,

Table 3 Panel regressions of strong leader perceptions on the GE and FS indexes (without time lags)[23]

DV: Country mean: Against strong leadership (0–1)	(1)	(2)	(3)	(4)
Country mean: GE index (0–1)	0.217	0.242		
	(0.22)	(0.15)		
Country mean: FS index (0–1)			0.462**	0.553***
			(0.14)	(0.13)
V-Dem electoral democracy index		−0.240***		−0.292***
		(0.06)		(0.06)
Real GDP per capita in 2011 USD		−0.000		−0.000**
		(0.00)		(0.00)
Country mean: Importance of God		−0.120		0.054
		(0.12)		(0.07)
Constant	0.438*	0.733***	0.344***	0.634***
	(0.18)	(0.08)	(0.09)	(0.08)
R2	0.327	0.415	0.438	0.553
N	74	73	74	73

*Standard errors in parentheses; * p < 0.05, ** p < 0.01, *** p < 0.001; fixed-effects panel models, robust standard errors, controlling for survey wave; WVS waves 3–7.*

---

[23] The negative coefficient for the electoral democracy index goes against our expectations about the relationship between democracy levels and a society's norms about strong political leadership. However, we suggest that this coefficient may be explained by the generally little across- and within-country variation in the electoral democracy index and potentially some democratic backsliding in some countries in the studied sample. Using random effects instead of fixed effects, and thereby allowing for cross-country variation, produces a null effect suggesting there is no significant relationship between the electoral democracy index and a society's norms about strong political leadership. However, given that we are interested in within-country variation and as suggested by the Hausman test (p-value: 0.0426), we stick to the fixed effects specification and acknowledge the unexpected direction of the relationship.

Table 4 Panel regression of the GE and FS indexes on strong leader perceptions (without time lags)

	(1) Country mean: GE index (0–1)	(2) Country mean: GE index (0–1)	(3) Country mean: FS index (0–1)	(4) Country mean: FS index (0–1)
Country mean: Against strong leadership (0–1)	0.135	0.185	0.412**	0.486**
	(0.11)	(0.11)	(0.13)	(0.15)
V-Dem electoral democracy index		0.135*		0.241***
		(0.06)		(0.06)
Real GDP per capita in 2011 USD		−0.000		0.000*
		(0.00)		(0.00)
Country mean: Importance of God		0.045		−0.248***
		(0.11)		(0.06)
Constant	0.694***	0.570***	0.319***	0.057
	(0.07)	(0.15)	(0.08)	(0.14)
R2	0.530	0.557	0.778	0.846
N	74	73	74	73

*Standard errors in parentheses; * $p < 0.05$ ** $p < 0.01$, *** $p < 0.001$; fixed-effects panel model, robust standard errors, controlling for survey wave; sample: OECD countries, WVS waves 3–7.*

wherein they act as both independent and dependent variables. However, the panel regression analyses reveal no significant relationship between GE norms and political (anti-)authoritarian norms. These models do not account for the respective other models and do not include time lags. Yet, they still support our theoretical argument for FS norms, while enabling us to use a greater sample of country-wave observations. They thus increase our confidence in the results presented in the previous SUR analyses (Tables 1 and 2), particularly on the relationship between FS norms and political (anti-)authoritarian norms.

The effect sizes for FS norms presented in the panel regressions are smaller in magnitude than those presented in the SUR analyses, yet still significant both in magnitude and in statistical terms (all p-values < 0.05). Table 3 shows that a one-unit increase in a country's FS norms is related to a 0.553-unit increase in the country's political anti-authoritarian norms (Model 4, p-value < 0.01), controlling for the country's state of democracy, GDP per capita and religiosity. Conversely, Table 4 shows that a one-unit increase in a country's political anti-authoritarian norms is related to 0.486-unit increase in the country's FS norms (Model 4, p-value < 0.001), controlling for our country-level control variables. To illustrate the implications of this effect size, a 0.486-unit increase equals moving from the most conservative observation in our sample, Turkey in survey wave 6 (FS index: 0.156), to a top-quartile progressive observation such as Spain in survey wave 6 (FS index: 0.647).

The previous results thus support the hypothesis of a mutually reinforcing relationship between a country's FS norms and its political (anti-)authoritarian norms. In all analyses, the FS index and political anti-authoritarianism are positively and significantly correlated, implying that stronger FS norms in a country are related to weaker political authoritarian norms, and vice versa. However, we do not find consistent evidence for a mutually reinforcing relationship between a country's GE norms and its political (anti-)authoritarian norms. Instead, our results support just one direction of influence on this front: stronger political (anti-)authoritarian norms are related to more conservative (progressive) GE norms. Thus, overall, the results suggest that positive shifts in FS norms are particularly important for strengthening political anti- authoritarian norms across this sample of economically advanced democracies. On the flip side, shifts toward political anti-authoritarian norms are particularly important not only for more progressive FS norms, but also GE norms. This implies that the current climate of rising political authoritarian leadership and attacks on GEFS that we observe in some of these countries could be particularly detrimental for continued progress in GEFS norms.

It is also important to note that our country-level results deviate from our individual-level results. When analyzing the variation across individuals, variation in GE values is more strongly related to variation in political authoritarian values when compared to FS values. As we speculate earlier, this may be explained by the fact that across our sample of countries and time points, we observe more variation in support for FS compared to GE, and, compared to the individual level, our number of observations is much more limited at the country level. This likely limits the potential impact of the GE index compared to the FS index on political (anti-)authoritarian norms at the country level. This is a drawback of working with country averages to measure the influence of the GE and FS norms on political (anti-)authoritarian norms across economically advanced democracies.

5 Conclusion

Throughout the past decade, various established democracies have observed a rise in politicization of gender and sexuality issues (Abou-Chadi, Breyer and Gessler 2021) along with a rise of authoritarian-leaning (radical) right-wing parties and political leaders. While there is variation across countries in how exactly these parties and leaders attack progressive understandings of gender and sexuality, the overall tendency to do so persists across various established democracies. Consequently, we have seen instances of dismantling of previously achieved women's and LGBTQI+ rights in several countries, as well as an increasingly dominant antifeminist political discourse in even more countries. This Element attempts to increase our understanding of these developments by developing a theory of rejection and support of political authoritarian leadership from a gendered perspective and basing this on a thorough and novel examination of how GEFS attitudes and attitudes toward political authoritarianism are related at the individual level and the country level.

We theorize that individuals begin developing GEFS values through gender socialization early, during childhood, in the family and in the more local, community forms of education and norm socialization to which they are exposed over their lifecycles. Through that exposure to patriarchal or egalitarian structures in families and communities, individuals develop leadership ideals which influence the form of political leadership they find acceptable or even appealing. If their socialization is progressive, we argue that this will be reflected in their GEFS values and increase their opposition to political authoritarianism, because their GEFS socialization and values are incompatible with political authoritarianism as a system rooted in and sustained through conformity to hegemonic masculine dominance. We also argue that progressive GEFS socialization and values buttress individuals' opposition to political authoritarianism indirectly through strengthening support for pluralism, strengthening support for democratic socialization in households, and increasing rejection of the use of violence to control social relations in households.

Our individual-level analysis generates results consistent with this individual-level theory. Our findings show that FS and, particularly, GE values are comparatively strong predictors of opposition to political authoritarianism, with similarly strong effects as variables that should, by definition, be very closely related to opposing political authoritarianism such as individuals' support for civil rights. Clearly, individuals' GEFS values play an essential role in understanding their support for or rejection of political authoritarianism. People with more conservative GEFS values are more likely to support strong political leadership that is not subjected to regular elections or checks on the government. Further, we find that parts of this relationship are explained by the influence of people's progressive GEFS values on their support for pluralism, democratic socialization in households, and the rejection of the use of violence in households. While each of these effects is small, each of them contributes to our understanding of the mechanisms explaining why progressive GEFS values are key predictors of people's opposition to political authoritarianism. Yet, given the relatively small mediation effects, future research may investigate other potential mediating variables to further uncover the mechanisms explaining how individuals' GEFS values affect their support or rejection of political authoritarianism.

By developing new theory, generating new analyses and generating the first supportive evidence, this individual-level work increases our understanding of how and why GEFS values influence individuals' attitudes toward political authoritarianism. Complementing and expanding on this work at the individual level, we then turn to the country level and consider how GEFS norms and political authoritarian norms are related as mutually reinforcing cultural processes as countries experience shifts in these norms over time. In so doing, we begin by advancing the theory of how countries develop a culture of GEFS and (opposition to) political authoritarianism as mutually reinforcing cultural processes. In developing one direction of influence, we build on our individual-level theory and add to the relevant literature on political culture by developing a new mechanism through which GEFS norms strengthen democratic culture. We focus on the gendered nature of authoritarian political leadership and, consequently, the importance of gender norms in generating the support or rejection of authoritarian leadership among populations. We argue that populations with more progressive levels of GEFS norms are more likely to oppose leadership rooted in and legitimated by the patriarchal structures of hegemonic masculine dominance, and vice versa. Political authoritarianism is rooted in, legitimated by, and sustained by those structures, and, thus, progress in GEFS norms will strengthen norms resistant to that form of political leadership. Conversely, conservative GEFS norms should be more conducive to a political authoritarian culture in a society.

In addition, we develop a theory for understanding the reverse direction of influence. On this front, we argue that one way populations' authoritarian norms influence GEFS norms is through improving support of democratic institutionalization if populations become less authoritarian, or weakening support of democratic institutionalization if populations become more authoritarian. In addition to this, we chart new theoretical ground by developing a theory on how the shift in (anti-)authoritarian norms potentially influences GEFS norms through explicit mobilization for or against GE and FS by the actors empowered by this (anti-)authoritarian shift in democracies. Building on the literatures about social norm change through institutional signals, political elites, and cue-taking, as well as the normalization of the radical right, we outline mechanisms explaining how political elites who challenge GEFS norms in conservative or progressive ways can affect GEFS norms in the population. Combined, our theories of the two directions of influence outline a theoretical framework for expecting a mutually reinforcing relationship between a country's population's GEFS norms and its political (anti-)authoritarian norms.

Having developed this theory, we then generate new analyses and new evidence consistent with this expectation of a mutually reinforcing relationship between FS norms and political (anti-)authoritarian norms but not between GE norms and political (anti-)authoritarian norms. Taking advantage of the panel data structure that we have at the country level, we find that a country's FS norms at one time point significantly affect its political (anti-)authoritarian norms at a subsequent time point, approximately five years later. Conversely, a country's political (anti-)authoritarian norms at one time point significantly affect both its FS and GE norms, approximately five years later. Overall, the results suggest that progressive shifts in FS norms are particularly important for strengthening political (anti-)authoritarian norms across this sample of economically advanced democracies. On the flip side, shifts toward political anti-authoritarian norms are particularly important not only for more progressive FS norms, but also for GE norms. This implies that the current climate of rising political authoritarian leadership and attacks on GEFS that we observe in some of these countries could be particularly detrimental for continued progress in GEFS norms.

Taking our individual-level and country-level analyses together, our results are inconsistent across the different levels. When analyzing the variation across individuals, variation in GE values is more strongly related to variation in political (anti-)authoritarian values, compared to variation in FS values. And, yet, in our country-level analysis, we do not find that a country's GE norms influence its political (anti-)authoritarian norms around five years later. Instead, our results support just one direction of influence on this front: political (anti-)authoritarian norms are related to GE norms around five years later. This may be explained by the fact that across our sample of countries and time points, we observe more variation in support for FS compared to GE, and, compared to the individual level, our number of observations is much more limited at the country level. This likely limits the potential impact of the GE index compared to the FS index on political (anti-)authoritarian attitudes at the country level. This is a drawback of working with country averages to measure the influence of the GE and FS norms on political (anti-)authoritarian norms across economically advanced democracies. We would pick up more variation in these norms, particularly in GE norms, with more nuanced regional data that captured the variation in these norms within countries. This more nuanced variation would align better with our theoretical expectations that the gender structures that individuals are embedded in vary profoundly at the more local, community level.

That noted, the inconsistency in results between the individual level and the country level is puzzling and calls for more research. We would particularly like to see research on this working with data on these norms across more local, community units within countries. We would also like to see future research collect and examine panel data at the individual level and investigate how consistency or changes in an individual's GEFS attitudes is related to consistency or change in their attitudes toward political authoritarianism over their lifecycle and how that is affected by the gender structures of the households and communities in which they are embedded. In addition, it could be worthwhile for future research to examine how recently observed gaps among the youngest generation of women and men in economically advanced democracies in support for gender equality potentially carry implications for gaps between young women and men in resistance to authoritarian leaning political leadership in those democracies. The more recent observation that young men are significantly less supportive of advancements in gender equality (Off et al. 2022) could have implications for increasing the mobilization of their support for authoritarian-leaning political leaders in economically advanced democracies.

Moreover, future research may collect and analyze country-level data to capture the theorized mechanisms that remain largely untested at the country level. Along these lines, future research might attempt to observe how the shift in (anti-)authoritarian norms potentially influences GEFS norms through explicit mobilization for or against GE and FS by the actors empowered by this (anti-)authoritarian shift in democracies. Is there evidence that this affects these social norm changes through institutional signals, political elites, and cue-taking?

This Element also carries important implications for the focus of research on political authoritarianism. Based on our theory and findings, as well as the many examples of authoritarian-leaning political leaders' attacks on GE and FS, research on political authoritarianism should take into account the strongly gendered nature of political authoritarianism as one of its important defining characteristics, and the potential consequences it can have. Much authoritarianism research frames the phenomenon as gender-neutral or does not refer to its gendered nature at all. This Element suggests that political authoritarianism is a strongly gendered phenomenon and should be considered as such.

Finally, this Element carries implications for the real world by contributing to explanations of the attacks on GE and FS by authoritarian-leaning political leaders that we have most strikingly observed in economically advanced democracies such as the United States, Hungary, or Poland. Our research suggests that resistance to these attacks on the socialization of progressive GEFS values and norms is vital to safeguarding democracy by maintaining and strengthening populations' opposition to political authoritarianism.

References

Aaldering, Loes and Daphne J. Van Der Pas (2020). "Political leadership in the media: Gender bias in leader stereotypes during campaign and routine times," *British Journal of Political Science*, 50(3), pp. 911–931.

Abou-Chadi, Tarik, Magdalena Breyer and Theresa Gessler (2021). "The (re)politicisation of gender in Western Europe," *European Journal of Politics and Gender*, 4(2), pp. 311–314.

Abou-Chadi, Tarik and Werner Krause (2018). "The causal effect of radical right success on mainstream parties' policy positions: A regression discontinuity approach," *British Journal of Political Science*, 50, pp. 829–847.

Adorno, Theodor, Else Frenkel-Brenswik, Daniel J. Levinson, and R. Nevitt Sanford (1950). *The authoritarian personality*. Verso Books (2019 ed.).

AfD (2016). *Grundsatzprogramm für Deutschland*, www.afd.de/grundsatzprogramm/.

Akkerman, Tjitske (2015). "Gender and the radical right in Western Europe: A comparative analysis of policy agendas," *Patterns of Prejudice*, 49(1–2), pp. 37–60.

Akrami, Nazar, Bo Ekehammar, and Fan Yang-Wallentin (2011). "Personality and social psychology factors explaining sexism," *Journal of Individual Differences*, 32(3), pp. 153–160.

Alexander, Amy C. (2012). "Change in women's descriptive representation and the belief in women's ability to govern: A virtuous cycle," *Politics & Gender*, 8(4), pp. 437–464.

Alexander, Amy C., and Christian Welzel (2011). "Measuring effective democracy: The human empowerment approach", *Comparative Politics*, 43(3), pp. 271–289.

Alexander, Amy C. and Christian Welzel (2017). *The myth of deconsolidation: Rising liberalism and the populist reaction*. ILE Working Paper Series No. 10, University of Hamburg, Institute of Law and Economics.

Altemeyer, Bob (1983). *Right-wing authoritarianism*. University of Manitoba Press.

Altemeyer, Bob (2007). *The authoritarians*. B. Altemeyer Winnipeg.

Andersen, Thomas B. (2023). Does democracy cause gender equality? *Journal of Institutional Economics*, 19(2), pp. 210–228.

Arias, Eric (2019). "How does media influence social norms? Experimental evidence on the role of common knowledge," *Political Science Research and Methods*, 7(3), pp. 561–578.

References

Austin, Darren E. J. and Mervyn Jackson (2019). "Benevolent and hostile sexism differentially predicted by facets of right-wing authoritarianism and social dominance orientation," *Personality and Individual Differences*, 139, pp. 34–38.

Baniamin, Hasan Muhammad (2022). "Variations in the acceptance of parental corporal punishment of children: What matters?" *Journal of Interpersonal Violence*, 37(19–20), NP18006–NP18031.

Barker, David C., and James D. Tinnick (2006). "Competing visions of parental roles and ideological constraint." *American Political Science Review*, 100(2), pp. 249–263.

Baron, Reuben M. and David A. Kenny (1986). "The moderator–mediator variable distinction in social psychological research: Conceptual, strategic, and statistical considerations," *Journal of Personality and Social Psychology*, 51(6), pp. 1173–1182.

Beer, Caroline (2009). "Democracy and gender equality", *Studies in Comparative International Development*, 44(3), pp. 212–227.

Ben-Ghiat, Ruth (2020). *Strongmen: Mussolini to the present*. WW Norton.

Bicchieri, Cristina (2016). *Norms in the wild: How to diagnose, measure, and change social norms*. Oxford University Press.

Bjork-James, Sophie (2020). "Racializing misogyny: Sexuality and gender in the new online white nationalism", *Feminist Anthropology*, 1(2), pp. 176–183.

Brunkert, Lennart, Stefan Kruse, and Christian Welzel (2019). "A tale of culture-bound regime evolution: The centennial democratic trend and its recent reversal", *Democratization*, 26(3), pp. 422–443.

Bystrov, Evgenia (2014). "Testing the second demographic transition theory with seemingly unrelated regression: Marital postponement and human empowerment," *European Sociological Review*, 30(4), pp. 483–499.

Cassese, Erin C. and Tiffany D. Barnes (2019). "Reconciling sexism and women's support for republican candidates: A look at gender, class, and whiteness in the 2012 and 2016 presidential races," *Political Behavior*, 41(3), pp. 677–700.

Chamorro Coneo, Ana M., Maria C. Navarro, and Nathalia Quiroz Molinares (2023). "Sexual-specific disgust sensitivity mechanisms in homonegativity and transnegativity; the mediating role of right-wing authoritarianism (RWA)," *Psychology & Sexuality*, 14(1), pp. 203–218.

Chenoweth, Erica and Zoe Marks (2022). "Revenge of the Patriarchs: Why Autocrats Fear Women," *Foreign Affairs*, 101(2), pp. 103–116.

Christopher, Andrew N. and Mark R. Wojda (2008). "Social dominance orientation, right-wing authoritarianism, sexism, and prejudice toward women in the workforce," *Psychology of Women Quarterly*, 32(1), pp. 65–73.

Christopher, Andrew N., Kevin L. Zabel and Drew E. Miller (2013). "Personality, Authoritarianism, Social Dominance, and Ambivalent Sexism: A Mediational Model," *Individual Differences Research*, 11(2), pp. 70–80.

Connell, Robert W. and James W. Messerschmidt (2005). "Hegemonic masculinity: Rethinking the concept," *Gender & Society*, 19(6), pp. 829–859.

Coppedge, Michael, John Gerring, Carl Henrik Knutsen et al. (2021). "V-Dem [Country– Year/Country–Date] Dataset v11.1", Varieties of Democracy (V-Dem) Project, https://doi.org/10.23696/vdemds21.

Dennison, James (2020). "How Issue Salience Explains the Rise of the Populist Right in Western Europe," *International Journal of Public Opinion Research*, 32(3), pp. 397–420.

Dietze, Gabriele and Julia Roth (2020). "Right-Wing Populism and Gender: A Preliminary Cartography of an Emergent Field of Research," in *Right-Wing Populism and Gender: European Perspectives and beyond*. Bielefeld: transcript Verlag.

Down, Ian and Kyung J. Han (2020). "Marginalisation or legitimation? Mainstream party positioning on immigration and support for radical right parties," *West European Politics*, 43(7), pp. 1388–1414.

Druckman, James N., Erik Peterson and Rune Slothuus (2013). "How elite partisan polarization affects public opinion formation," *American Political Science Review*, 107(1), pp. 57–79.

Duncan, Lauren E. (2006). "What feminist and political psychologists can learn from each other: The case of authoritarianism," *Feminism & Psychology*, 16(1), pp. 58–64.

Duncan, Lauren E., Bill E. Peterson and David G. Winter (1997). "Authoritarianism and gender roles: Toward a psychological analysis of hegemonic relationships," *Personality and Social Psychology Bulletin*, 23(1), pp. 41–49.

Eckhardt, William (1991). "Authoritarianism," *Political Psychology*, 12(1), pp. 97–124.

Engelhardt, Andrew M., Stanley Feldman and Marc J. Hetherington (2023). "Advancing the measurement of authoritarianism," *Political Behavior*, 45(2), pp. 537–560.

Feinberg, Matthew, and Elisabeth Wehling (2018). "A moral house divided: How idealized family models impact political cognition", *PLOS One*, 13(4), p. e0193347.

Feldman, Stanley (2003). "Enforcing social conformity: A theory of authoritarianism," *Political Psychology*, 24(1), pp. 41–74.

Feldman, Stanley and Karen Stenner (1997). "Perceived threat and authoritarianism," *Political Psychology*, 18(4), pp. 741–770.

Foa, Roberto S., Yascha Mounk., and Andrew Klassen (2022). "Why the future cannot be predicted", *Journal of Democracy*, 33(1), 147–155.

FPÖ (2011). *Party Programme of the Freedom Party of Austria (FPÖ)*, www.fpoe.at/fileadmin/user_upload/www.fpoe.at/dokumente/2015/2011_graz_parteiprogramm_englisch_web.pdf.

Geva, Dorit (2020). "Daughter, mother, captain: Marine Le Pen, gender, and populism in the French National Front," *Social Politics: International Studies in Gender, State & Society*, 27(1), pp. 1–26.

Hicks, Raymond and Dustin Tingley (2011). "Causal mediation analysis," *The Stata Journal*, 11(4), pp. 605–619.

Hooghe, Liesbet, Gary Marks and Carole Wilson (2002). "Does left/right structure party positions on European integration?" *Comparative Political Studies*, 35(8), pp. 965–989.

Hyde, Janet Shibley, Rebecca S. Bigler, Daphna Joel, Charlotte Chucky Tate, and Sari M. van Anders (2019). "The future of sex and gender in psychology: Five challenges to the gender binary." *American Psychologist*, 74(2), 171–193.

Iacobucci, Dawn, Neela Saldanha and Xiaoyan Deng (2007). "A meditation on mediation: Evidence that structural equations models perform better than regressions," *Journal of Consumer Psychology*, 17(2), pp. 139–153.

Imai, Kosuke, Luke Keele and Dustin Tingley (2010). "A general approach to causal mediation analysis," *Psychological Methods*, 15(4), p. 309.

Inglehart, Ronald and Pippa Norris (2003). *Rising tide: Gender equality and cultural change around the world*. Cambridge University Press.

Inglehart, Ronald, Pippa Norris, and Christian Welzel (2003). "Gender equality and democracy," in Inglehart, Ronald (ed.) *Human values and social change*. Brill, pp. 91–115.

Inglehart, Ronald and Christian Welzel (2005). *Modernization, cultural change, and democracy: The human development sequence*. Cambridge University Press.

Inglehart, Ronald, Christian Haerpfer, Alejandro Moreno et al. (eds.) (2020). World Values Survey: All Rounds – Country-Pooled Datafile. Madrid, Spain & Vienna, Austria: JD Systems Institute & WVSA Secretariat, www.worldvaluessurvey.org/WVSDocumentationWVL.jsp.

Jennings, M. Kent and Richard G. Niemi (2015). *Political character of adolescence: The influence of families and schools*. Princeton University Press.

Jennings, M. Kent, Laura Stoker and Jake Bowers (2009). "Politics across generations: Family transmission reexamined," *The Journal of Politics*, 71(3), pp. 782–799.

Kaul, Nitasha (2021). "The misogyny of authoritarians in contemporary democracies," *International Studies Review*, 23(4), pp. 1619–1645.

Kirsch, Helen, and Christian Welzel (2019). "Democracy misunderstood: Authoritarian notions of democracy around the globe", *Social Forces*, 98, pp. 59–92.

Korolczuk, Elżbieta and Agnieszka Graff (2018). "Gender as 'Ebola from Brussels': The anticolonial frame and the rise of illiberal populism," *Signs: Journal of Women in Culture and Society*, 43(4), pp. 797–821.

Krook, Mona Lena (2020). *Violence against women in politics*. Oxford University Press.

Kuhar, Roman and David Paternotte (2018). *Anti-gender campaigns in Europe: Mobilizing against Equality*. Rowman & Littlefield International.

Lakoff, George (1996). *Moral politics: What conservatives know that liberals don't*. University of Chicago Press.

Leeper, Thomas J. and Slothuus, Rune (2014). "Political parties, motivated reasoning, and public opinion formation," *Political Psychology*, 35(1), pp. 129–156.

Lindskog, Hilma and Maria Oskarson (2022). "Generational differences in disguise? A longitudinal study of the liberalising effect of education on socio-cultural attitudes," *West European Politics*, 46(3), pp. 500–525.

Lomazzi, Vera (2023). The cultural roots of violence against women: individual and institutional gender norms in 12 countries. *Social Sciences*, 12(3), 117.

Mallinas, Stephanie R., Jarret T. Crawford and Jeremy A. Frimer (2020). "Subcomponents of right-wing authoritarianism differentially predict attitudes toward obeying authorities," *Social Psychological and Personality Science*, 11(1), pp. 134–143.

Manne, Kate (2017). *Down girl: The logic of misogyny*. Oxford University Press.

Meret, Susi (2015). "Charismatic female leadership and gender: Pia Kjærsgaard and the Danish People's Party," *Patterns of Prejudice*, 49(1–2), pp. 81–102.

Merkel, Wolfgang and Anna Lührmann (2021). "Resilience of democracies: Responses to illiberal and authoritarian challenges," *Democratization*, 28(5), pp. 869–884.

Miklikowska, Marta, and Hurme, Helena (2011). "Democracy begins at home: Democratic parenting and adolescents' support for democratic values", *European Journal of Developmental Psychology*, 8(5), 541–557.

Miller, Patrick R., Andrew R. Flores, Donald P. Haider-Markel et al. (2017). "Transgender politics as body politics: Effects of disgust sensitivity and authoritarianism on transgender rights attitudes," *Politics, Groups, and Identities*, 5(1), pp. 4–24.

Mudde, Cas (2007). *Populist radical right parties in Europe*. Cambridge University Press.

Norris, Pippa (2017). "Is Western democracy backsliding? Diagnosing the risks," *The Journal of Democracy* (Web Exchange).

Norris, Pippa and Ronald Inglehart (2019). *Cultural backlash: Trump, Brexit, and authoritarian populism*. Cambridge University Press.

OECD (2024). *2024 Annual Update on OECD Standard-Setting*, https://legalinstruments.oecd.org/en/about.

Off, Gefjon (2023). "Complexities and nuances in radical right voters' (anti) feminism," *Social Politics: International Studies in Gender, State & Society*, 30(2), pp. 607–629.

Off, Gefjon, Nicholas Charron, and Amy Alexander (2022). "Who perceives women's rights as threatening to men and boys? Explaining modern sexism among young men in Europe," *Frontiers in Political Science*, 4, pp. 1–15.

Oyamot Jr, Clifton M., Melinda S. Jackson, Emily L. Fisher Grace Deason and Eugene Borgida (2017). "Social norms and egalitarian values mitigate authoritarian intolerance toward sexual minorities," *Political Psychology*, 38(5), pp. 777–794.

Peterson, Bill E. and Eileen L. Zurbriggen (2010). "Gender, sexuality, and the authoritarian personality," *Journal of Personality*, 78(6), pp. 1801–1826.

Petersen, Michael B., Martin Skov, Søren Serritzlew and Thomas Ramsøy (2013). "Motivated reasoning and political parties: Evidence for increased processing in the face of party cues," *Political Behavior*, 35(4), pp. 831–854.

Pless, Anna, Paul Tromp, and Dick Houtman (2021). "Religious and secular value divides in Western Europe: A cross-national comparison (1981–2008)," *International Political Science Review*, 44(2), pp. 178–194.

Pratto, Felicia, Jim Sidanius, Lisa M. Stallworth and Bertram F. Malle (1994). "Social dominance orientation: A personality variable predicting social and political attitudes," *Journal of Personality and Social Psychology*, 67(4), pp. 741–763.

Rawłuszko, Marta (2019). "And if the opponents of gender ideology are right? Gender politics, Europeanization, and the democratic deficit," *Politics & Gender*, 17(2), pp. 301–323.

Ridgeway, Cecilia L. (2009). "Framed before we know it: How gender shapes social relations," *Gender & Society*, 23(2), pp. 145–160.

Russell, Brenda L. and Kristin Y. Trigg (2004). "Tolerance of sexual harassment: An examination of gender differences, ambivalent sexism, social dominance, and gender roles," *Sex Roles*, 50(7), pp. 565–573.

Ryan, Michelle K., Alexander S. Haslam, Mette D. Hersby, Renata Bongiorno (2011). "Think crisis–think female: The glass cliff and contextual variation in the think manager–think male stereotype," *Journal of Applied Psychology*, 96(3), p. 470.

Sartori, Giovanni (1997). "Understanding pluralism," *Journal of Democracy*, 8(4), pp. 58–69.

Sauer, Birgit (2020). "Authoritarian right-wing populism as masculinist identity politics. The role of affects," in Dietze, G. and Roth, J. (eds.) *Right-wing populism and gender: European perspectives and beyond*. Transcript Verlag, pp. 23–40.

Seguino, Stephanie (2011). "Help or hindrance? Religion's impact on gender inequality in attitudes and outcomes," *World Development*, 39(8), 1308–1321.

Sibley, Chris G., Mark S. Wilson and John Duckitt (2007). "Antecedents of men's hostile and benevolent sexism: The dual roles of social dominance orientation and right-wing authoritarianism," *Personality and Social Psychology Bulletin*, 33(2), pp. 160–172.

Slothuus, Rune and De Vreese, Claes H. (2010). "Political parties, motivated reasoning, and issue framing effects," *The Journal of Politics*, 72(3), pp. 630–645.

Spierings, Niels (2020). "Why gender and sexuality are both trivial and pivotal in populist radical right politics," in Dietze, G. and Roth, J. (eds.) *Right-wing populism and gender*. Transcript-Verlag, pp. 41–58.

Stenner, Karen (2005). *The authoritarian dynamic*. Cambridge University Press.

Stockard, Jean (2006). "Gender socialization," in Saltzman Chafetz, J. (ed.) *Handbook of the Sociology of Gender*. Kluwer Academic/Plenum Publishers, pp. 215–227.

Tankard, Margaret E. and Elizabeth L. Paluck (2016). "Norm perception as a vehicle for social change," *Social Issues and Policy Review*, 10(1), pp. 181–211.

Teorell, Jan, Aksel Sundström, Sören Holmberg et al. (2023). The quality of government standard dataset, version January 23. University of Gothenburg: The Quality of Government Institute, www.gu.se/en/quality-government doi:10.18157/qogstdjan23.

Valentim, Vicente (2021). "Parliamentary representation and the normalization of radical right support," *Comparative Political Studies*, 54(14), pp. 2475–2511.

Vox (2023). *Programa Electoral Para Las Elecciones Electorales*, www.vox espana.es/programa/programa-electoral-vox.

Weeks, Ana and Peter Allen (2022). "Backlash against 'identity politics': Far right success and mainstream party attention to identity groups," *Politics, Groups, and Identities*, 11(5), pp. 935935–953.

Welzel, Christian (2006). "Democratization as an emancipative process: The neglected role of mass motivations," *European Journal of Political Research*, 45(6), pp. 871–896.

Welzel, Christian (2013). *Freedom Rising*. Cambridge University Press.

Welzel, Christian (2014). "Evolution, empowerment, and emancipation: How societies climb the freedom ladder," *World Development*, 64, pp. 33–51.

Welzel, Christian, Stefan Kruse, and Lennart Brunkert (2022). "Why the future is (still) democratic," *Journal of Democracy*, 33(1), pp. 156–162.

Yuval-Davis, Nira (1997). *Gender and Nation*. Sage.

Zaller, John R. (1992). *The nature and origins of mass opinion*. Cambridge University Press.

Cambridge Elements

Gender and Politics

Tiffany D. Barnes
University of Texas at Austin

Tiffany D. Barnes is Professor of Political Science at the University of Texas at Austin. She is the author of *Women, Politics, and Power: A Global Perspective* (Rowman & Littlefield, 2007) and, award-winning, *Gendering Legislative Behavior* (Cambridge University Press, 2016). Her research has been funded by the National Science Foundation (NSF) and recognized with numerous awards. Barnes is the former president of the Midwest Women's Caucus and founder and director of the Empirical Study of Gender (EGEN) network.

Diana Z. O'Brien
Washington University in St. Louis

Diana Z. O'Brien is the Bela Kornitzer Distinguished Professor of Political Science at Washington University in St. Louis. She specializes in the causes and consequences of women's political representation. Her award-winning research has been supported by the NSF and published in leading political science journals. O'Brien has also served as a Fulbright Visiting Professor, an associate editor at *Politics & Gender*, the president of the Midwest Women's Caucus, and a founding member of the EGEN network.

About the Series

From campaigns and elections to policymaking and political conflict, gender pervades every facet of politics. Elements in Gender and Politics features carefully theorized, empirically rigorous scholarship on gender and politics. The Elements both offer new perspectives on foundational questions in the field and identify and address emerging research areas.

Cambridge Elements

Gender and Politics

Elements in the Series

In Love and at War: Marriage in Non-state Armed Groups
Hilary Matfess

Counter-Stereotypes and Attitudes Toward Gender and LGBTQ Equality
Jae-Hee Jung and Margit Tavits

The Politics of Bathroom Access and Exclusion in the United States
Sara Chatfield

Women, Gender, and Rebel Governance during Civil Wars
Meredith Maloof Loken

Abortion Attitudes and Polarization in the American Electorate
Erin C. Cassese, Heather L. Ondercin and Jordan Randall

Gender, Ethnicity, and Intersectionality in Cabinets: Asia and Europe in Comparative Perspective
Amy H. Liu, Roman Hlatky, Keith Padraic Chew, Eoin L. Power, Sam Selsky, Betty Compton and Meiying Xu

Gendered Jobs and Local Leaders: Women, Work, and the Pipeline to Local Political Office
Rachel Bernhard and Mirya R. Holman

What's Happened to the Gender Gap in Political Activity?: Social Structure, Politics, and Participation in the United States
Shauna L. Shames, Sara Morell, Ashley Jardina, Kay Lehman Schlozman and Nancy Burns

Family Matters: How Romantic Partners Shape Politicians' Careers
Olle Folke, Moa Frödin Gruneau and Johanna Rickne

Glass Ceilings, Glass Cliffs, and Quicksands: Gendered Party Leadership in Parliamentary Systems
Andrea S. Aldrich and Zeynep Somer-Topcu

Attitudes toward Political Authoritarianism in Economically Advanced Democracies: The Role of Gender Values and Norms
Amy C. Alexander and Gefjon Off

A full series listing is available at: www.cambridge.org/EGAP

Printed by Libri Plureos GmbH in Hamburg, Germany